PRAISE FOR BREAKING FREE

"Dreams turn into hope when we bring useful action to the work. Shannon Talbot's book is a powerful step on that journey."

-Seth Godin, *author of The Song of Significance*

"I love this book. Shannon Talbot's focus on authenticity hits the mark. Your life or career can be a source of pride or a source of frustration, a lifelong adrenalin rush or a source of anxiety. This book makes it very clear: it's your choice."

-Pattie Lovett-Reid,
former chief financial commentator, CTV News

"Shannon Talbot takes us on a personal journey of how she defines success, and breaks it down into easy to manage steps we can incorporate into our own lives, no matter how old we are or where we are in our own journey. Through a series of anecdotes, self-reflections and exercises, Shannon will have you facing your fears, and turning your dreams into goals. Knowing when to set boundaries and when to ask for help is a learned skill Shannon helps to uncover. Her book is a great guide for those struggling to get to the next level of success and happiness, personally and professionally."

-Kathy Buckworth, *author of I Am So The Boss of You*

"There are very few secrets to take away from self-help books, unless they come from a place of honesty and therefore authenticity. Shannon Talbot talks about the circumstances she faced trying to doing it all and the price she paid and the lessons she learned along the way. The first two words of her title say it all - Breaking Free. She did, and in this book she gives you the wings to stop holding back and to start being you."

-Tony Chapman, *host of the podcast Chatter that Matters*

"Get ready to finally take that step toward the person you have always wanted to be! Shannon Talbot offers a straightforward approach to cutting the crap, setting a vision and designing the life you deserve."

-Stuart Knight, *author, speaker and founder of The Human Connection Group*

BREAKING FREE

STOP HOLDING BACK, START BEING YOU—
YOUR GUIDE TO CREATING THE CAREER
AND LIFE OF YOUR DREAMS

SHANNON TALBOT

For Chris, Jackson & Zachary. Thank you for supporting and motivating me to chase my dreams and for listening to the many, many stories of inspiring people I studied while writing this book. I love you to the moon and beyond.

And for Jack, my dear father-in-law who passed away while I was writing this book. Thank you for encouraging me to go after what I wanted in life.

CONTENTS

"Let no one cage who you were born to be."
–Anonymous

HOW IT STARTED

Isn't it funny how sometimes just one conversation can change our lives?

One conversation with a person, good or bad, can stay with you for years. Perhaps it determined where you went to school, your style, which career path you chose. Perhaps it's why you might not know just how great you are or never realized your full potential–because someone took that from you. Maybe you wanted to be an artist, actor or musician as a kid, and a parent or teacher snuffed out your light, telling you "That's not a real career" or "You'll never be successful." Or perhaps it's the reason why you have such high expectations for yourself and excel at almost everything you do, because people believed in you.

For me, it was hearing this: "Shannon, I can see you being Prime Minister one day."

For a nine-year-old living in Canada, that was a pretty awesome compliment to receive. And one that has stayed with me until now, at age 42.

As you might have guessed, I never did become Prime Minister. Heck, I can't even imagine being a member of Parliament (no offence to anyone who is). Politics is just not an area I'm passionate about. But what that compliment did do was give me the confidence to aim high. To dream big and to take action on those dreams. And the best part is, the compliment was from the receptionist at the foot doctor's office where I went to get a wart burnt off my foot (yup, gross). I have no idea what we talked about or what I said to her in the waiting room that inspired her to say that, or even if it's just something she says to every kid who comes in, but it didn't matter. She gave me hope.

And now I want to give it to you: Hope. In the form of inspiring real-life stories from incredible everyday people I've interviewed for this book, along with some practical how-to action steps and exercises to take that hope and turn it into real, tangible results, which can turn your dreams from imaginary to real.

But first, I want to take you back a few years to when I finally understood what lit me up and the path it took to get me there, since that's when I really leaned on the hope that I was destined to do something more meaningful to me than I'd been doing.

My earliest definition of success came from The Game of Life, a board game from the '90s where you spin a wheel to travel from early adulthood to retirement and experience different milestones along the way. It's a game where I'd defined my jackpot cards as going to university, becoming a lawyer, making $50,000, having a house, getting married and having four kids.

In 2019, I would have looked like I had won the game—I had the incredible husband and kids, a house by the beach, the dog, the university degrees, a great job and income and wonderful friends and family.

But I hadn't won.

As great as things looked on paper, something was missing. I had spent years so focused on having a family and climbing the corporate ladder that I no longer knew what made me tick. When I was burning out at a company from working long hours, and from stress and anxiety, I'd change jobs. I acted how I thought I should act for people to get ahead at work and for people to like me. And I was motivated by external validation—if someone told me I was doing a great job, I felt happy. If not, it fueled me to try harder.

I hadn't grown up thinking I would become a banker—shocking, I know! But I got a job working for a bank branch during university, and then ended up rising through the corporate ranks at bank head offices for 15 years. While this experience made me who I am today and was a blast for the most part, it wasn't a career path that truly lit me up.

It would take spending 31 days in the hospital with my eldest son, who was then only five and suffering from a perforated appendix, for me to step back and take a hard look at my life.

Watching him sleep in his hospital bed, I asked myself three questions: Am I happy? Am I healthy? Do I feel fulfilled?

My answers were "Meh, not really." And that was followed by guilt. How could I not be happy with all that I had? What more did I want? I wasn't sure but knew I had to find out. I also realized that I had been feeling this way for a long time. Upon leaving the hospital with a healthy son, I set out on a journey to answer a big heck yeah to my three questions.

My first step on that journey was to figure out what would light me up professionally, so I signed up for a three-day retreat with an executive coach. Little did I know that I would leave that retreat with a dream. A dream that would be summed up with one sentence—*I am a successful entrepreneur who helps others to live happier, healthier and more fulfilling lives.* It's a line I created after finally admitting that I was allowed to change my dreams and my definition of success.

I gave myself 10 years to fulfill that dream and, in the meantime, I switched industries from banking to advertising, going from a Senior Manager to a Vice President role. There, I felt more inspired, creative and strategic. I loved fostering my team to see them develop and grow. I enjoyed presenting to clients. The hours were long and the stress was constant, though, leading my youngest to ask me if he could give me a goal for the year. He asked me if I could "be less angry this year" as I was "angry all the time." His goal was like a knife to my chest but that was the push I needed to truly prioritize my health, happiness and fulfillment.

I went from practically never exercising to running three 10 km races and moving my body on a regular basis. I practised ways to better manage my stress and anxiety so I wouldn't be so angry. And I learned to be more present with my kids and husband (although that is definitely still a work in progress). *And* I took the coaching certifications I needed to launch my business.

I can confidently tell you that I am now a successful entrepreneur who helps others to live happier, healthier and more fulfilling lives. I have the life I envisioned years ago, where I get to walk my kids to and from school, have more autonomy in my work, and do things like public speaking, leadership coaching and writing, which truly light me up in ways better than I ever imagined. I also have the tools to overcome what used to hold me back: things like strategies for how to manage my stress and anxiety, and the habits required to live a more authentic and happier life.

I now say a big heck yes to feeling happier, healthier and fulfilled.

But it wasn't easy to get here. First, I had to set the vision for my future. I had to take responsibility and realize that it was up to me to make my dreams come true. Along the way, I had to uncover and face what held me back: the BS, fears, excuses, beliefs and bad habits. I had to muster the courage, embrace the discomfort and take action to overcome these obstacles. Really, I had to get out of my own way and break free.

And this is what I want to share with you.

This book is for you if you feel stuck in your career or life. If you've been holding back at work or at home. If you feel something is missing but you're not sure what it is or how to get it. If you have big dreams that scare the crap out of you. If you're done playing small and want to feel more satisfied in your life. If you want to say a big heck yes to living the life of your dreams.

This book is not about telling you how to rise the corporate ranks and become a CEO before you're 40. Unless you want to. If that is your dream, this book will help you get there. But if your dream is to work less and be more present with family and friends, that's awesome too. This book will also help you.

I've filled this book with my personal stories of rejection, failure and loss. I talk about the challenges of being a mom with an ambitious career and burning out. More importantly, I share how I overcame the obstacles that were holding me back from living a dream life that seemed both scary and silly.

I also share inspiring real-life stories of women who overcame big obstacles to live their dream lives. Women who have overcome things like being let go, starting a new business, and fear of speaking up in a meeting. Women who have learned to rise through the corporate ranks without sacrificing their well-being or family, as well as how to get a promotion or raise, focus on their health, and balance raising kids with their own personal ambitions.

Essentially, I wrote the book I wish someone had given me to help me navigate my career: A guide to creating the vision for what a successful life looks like to you, identifying what obstacles might get in your way, breaking free from these obstacles and learning how to keep going, especially when life throws you a curveball or 10.

I've also included exercises to help get you closer to making your dreams a reality. You don't have to stop reading and complete the exercises in order to move on to the next chapter. You might prefer reading the whole book first and then coming back and completing the exercises at a pace that works for you. Some exercises might seem more relevant to you and where you're at right now, and others you might want to skip and come back to later. That's okay; make this book work for you. Just remember, you get what you put in.

As my coaching clients will share, as much as we may dread doing exercises or be tempted to skip them, they may be just the thing that helps you get over your obstacles. If you approach them with curiosity, you might be amazed at where you land one year from now.

I must warn you though, it will take work. It can get messy, and at times you may feel like you're moving backwards not forwards, but if you stick with it, you will get there. I'm living proof and so are many of the women I've had the pleasure of working with in my practice. Just one small step towards your dreams can have a bigger impact than you realize.

If you are up for it, this book will serve as your compass, leading you towards a life that's not only more fulfilling but also more fun, exciting and authentically YOU.

Now get ready to break free from what's been holding you back so you can embrace the life you're meant to live, and experience true happiness and success along the way. It's your time to soar.

WHAT LIGHTS US UP

"The path from dreams to success does exist. May you have the vision to find it, the courage to get on to it, and the perseverance to follow it."

–Kalpana Chawla,
Indian-American astronaut and aerospace engineer

How many times have you heard it: Dreams are for kids. You need to be realistic with your life. Settle down, buy a house, have a stable income. Work at the same company long enough to get a good pension.

As an adult, it can be hard to remember what lights us up. We let fear, self-doubt and guilt hold us back. Perhaps that's why only 21% of employees feel engaged at work and just 33% of employees are thriving in their overall well-being.[1] We either feel stuck and unmotivated or we believe we can't go after our dreams–that we're too old or that it's selfish. And when we don't feel a sense of purpose or when we carry around the guilt of wanting to live a more meaningful life, we risk burning out.

Well, it's time to press delete on every negative thing you've ever heard or thought when it comes to chasing your dreams. The "You're too old,"

"It won't work," "It's not practical" lines you've been fed. Hopefully you are reading this book because you still have dreams you want to make a reality. Perhaps you know what lights you up but are afraid to chase it. Maybe you're not sure what you're passionate about yet but want to explore.

Whatever it is, now is your time to uncover what lights you up. It's your time to push logic and reason aside. Your time to dream big without holding back. Let yourself go to the exciting place of la-la land–or Disney World, if you prefer. The land where magical things happen and dreams come true. Your ticket awaits.

Dreams aren't just for kids

Since I was young, I've been fascinated with successful people. Athletes, CEOs, actors, musicians. Their stories inspire me. And one thing I've noticed that's true of the majority of them is that they dreamt big. They had to, otherwise their competition would have stepped right in and taken over. Can you imagine if Venus and Serena Williams, or their dad Richard for that matter, just thought, Oh, wouldn't it be nice if we played some tournaments outside of Compton and maybe won some? NO! That vision would have gotten them nowhere. They had to have the drive, the vision to succeed. They had to dream BIG.

Now, do I think we should all walk around thinking we're going to be the next Steve Jobs or Taylor Swift? Nope, but I do think we should give ourselves permission to dream as big as we'd like, plus the permission to fail while pursuing our dreams, as rarely does success come without failure. After we've tried our very best to succeed, then and only then should we consider changing our path or pivoting a little.

But so many of us don't even make it to that first step of going for it. We dream big and then immediately tell ourselves all the reasons why that dream is stupid or that we'll fail or that it's irresponsible. Or we share our dream with others who don't believe in it and we listen to them when they say it's not for us.

So, right now I am giving you full permission to tell logic, reasoning and any other doubts to get lost. And when they come back, as they inevitably will, you have my full permission to tell them to go to hell and get back to your dream.

Let's start by asking yourself: What age were you a dreamer?

Go back to that age and pretend you have the whole world ahead of you, and nothing can get in your way. Unless you're now 40 and your dream was to get into the WNBA–then you might want to think of another age and another dream.

I know you had big dreams at some point otherwise you likely wouldn't be reading this book. Was it when you were a child? A teenager? In college or university? Or perhaps it was more recent? In my case, I started a jewellery business while on university exchange in Peru. I liked the idea of being an entrepreneur, but in the end, I wasn't passionate enough about that particular business to overcome my fear of sales and I gave it up after a couple of years of half-heartedly working on it. The desire to own my own business, however, never went away.

Was there a goal or dream you once thought about pursuing but perhaps it wasn't the right path? Let yourself go back to the time when you were dreaming of something bigger, something more, something else. What did you dream about? What did you see for yourself? What were those goals?

If you start to hear those voices creeping in and telling you to forget when you were a dreamer, tell these voices to get lost. There is a time and place for those thoughts, and that is when your life is in danger, not when you're trying to reach your goals.

If you start to think about *how* something will happen or *when*, forget those thoughts too. We don't need to know the answers to those questions yet. Those things will happen. In time.

This book is about following your heart on whatever path *you* want to choose. If you want to become a Senior Vice President at the company you work for, fantastic. If you want to quit your job and become a stay-at-home mom, envision that! If you want to start a new company but have no idea how to do it, that's OK too. The how will come. What's more important than the how right now is the dream. Get crystal clear on what the dream looks and feels like. The first step on any journey is to have an idea of where you're going while understanding the path to get there will have unexpected twists and turns. Learning to embrace these twists and turns while keeping an eye on your destination are the keys to getting there.

This first exercise is all about possibilities and passion.

Ready to dive in? Let's go!

Exercise: What Lights You Up?

For this first exercise, you'll want to jot down notes so you can come back to them in future chapters.

If this were an audiobook (and yes I will delete this line in my audiobook version), I would invite you to close your eyes right now and take some big deep breaths. Inhale through the nose to the count of five, hold at the top for five and slowly exhale out the mouth for seven. Do this a few times and as you're doing it relax your forehead, jaw, shoulders, butt cheeks (we clench those way more than we know), hands and feet. Breathe out any stress or worries and breathe in fresh, exciting possibilities. Let go of any judgment you have of yourself and give yourself full permission to dream big. Imagine you are five years old and have yet to discover the world of why something is stupid or impractical.

I invite you to enter the world where anything is possible. That everything starts with an idea. And an idea combined with passion and motivation is all you need. Everything else can be learned as you go when you have the willingness to learn.

Now, picture your life in five years and your ideal, but typical, day. What are you doing from the time you wake up in the morning until you go to bed at night? I want you to imagine every single detail. What are your first thoughts in the morning? Are you with anyone? If so, who? What does your home look like? Where do you live? Think of your morning routine—what is it? How does it make you feel?

What activities fill your day? If work does, what does your workday entail? Where do you work? How do you get there? Who do you work with? How do you get along? Do you take breaks? How does your work make you feel? What do you do for lunch? What do you eat? What feels important about work—the money, the title, the impact, having a sense of purpose, the people, the work itself? What do you enjoy most? What is your ideal salary? How is your performance measured? How are you compensated?

After work, where do you go? How do you spend your evening? Do you have any hobbies? Are you by yourself or with others? What does dinner look like? What kind of clothes are you wearing? Who do you spend your time with? What's important about this time? Do you have a bedtime routine? If so, what is it?

Now, picture yourself looking in the mirror at the end of the night. What about this future self are you most proud of? What makes her happy? What message does she have for the current you? What are the last thoughts going through her head before she goes to bed?

Relish these feelings for a few moments. Dial them up really high, so they're super strong in your mind, body and heart. This is what you're setting yourself up for. This vision that can and will come true if you take steps to make it happen. Having belief in this vision and yourself is Step 1. And the way to build this belief is to revisit this vision every day. Write it down and say it out loud. (OK, saying it out loud may be uncomfortable, I get it, but do it anyway, even if it's a whisper to start.) Trust me, our subconscious is a powerful thing and the more messages we can send to it about our future, the more it will do its magic to support our journey. It's pretty incredible when you look at the stats and see that 97% of our actions are controlled by our subconscious[2]–97%! What that means is that what we tell ourselves is really darn important and the more we can picture success and our dream future, the greater chance we have of making it happen.

Getting crystal clear on your vision

Why is having a clear and exciting vision so important? Because, according to neuroscience research, mental simulations help people turn their thoughts into action. It's why elite athletes like NBA star LeBron James visualize every game in their head before they even step on to the court.

When we truly believe in something, we will do the hard work required. We will step outside of our comfort zone and take risks. Manifestation is not wishing for something to happen and then sitting around. That's luck. Manifestation is believing in something and then taking action.

As Henry Ford said, "Whether you think you can, or you think you can't–you're right." Your thoughts create your life.

In an interview with Reese Witherspoon[3], Sara Blakely, the founder of Spanx–you know, the women's shapewear attire company valued at over one billion dollars–shared that when she was 16, her dad had her listen to manifestation tapes in her car. Her friends would all run to get in anyone's car but Sara's, so they didn't have to listen to her tapes. Now, those same friends joke saying they wished they'd gone in her car given how successful she is today.

My own manifesting journey started in 2020 after reading Rachel Hollis' book *Girl, Stop Apologizing.* In it, she tells readers to write down the 10 dreams they want to accomplish within 10 years. At the time, my husband and I were in a rough patch, like many couples with two young kids and a lack of sleep are. One thing I wrote down was: *Chris and I have an exceptional marriage.* Short, but sweet.

Another dream I wrote down was: *I am a successful entrepreneur who helps people live happier, healthier and more fulfilling lives.* At the time, I was working in banking, my schooling was in business and my first thought was, Shannon, how the hell will you ever do that? You're not even close to being qualified to "help people." But this exercise isn't about the how or if the dream is realistic or not. It's about getting your dream out there. Full stop. It was my vision for 10 years down the road and that's what I saw for my career path.

Some of my dreams were related to my relationships with my kids, family and friends, some were related to my health, some my community and others were aspirational goals like owning a cottage and travelling the world.

What seemed the most far-fetched at the time were my career goals. As part of my journey to break free, I'd worked with executive and life coaches but not once did it cross my mind that I would ever be a coach myself. I still had no clue how I could "help people." I saw writing and speaking in my future, but the coaching part took a couple of years to come to life.

Instead, I decided that I wanted my next move to be a more senior role in an industry with super creative people doing something different than I'd ever done before. I had no idea what industry, company or role that could be so I followed Michelle Obama's example of how she switched careers and industries (more to come on that in a bit) and started networking to see what was out there, making note of what types of things interested me. With each conversation, I was able to create a list of the things I wanted in my next job.

Well wouldn't you know, I had a call with a recruiter shortly after my list was done and after telling him what I was looking for he told me he had the perfect job for me. I was intrigued. Then the recruiter told me it was for an advertising agency. Having worked on the client side with advertising agencies, I told him no, that wasn't something that interested me. I knew clients were demanding and hours were long. He asked me to hear him out and everything he shared with me did align with what I wanted: It was a VP role with a big team. It included some travel to the U.S. (to Chicago and New York, both cities I love). My client would be a large bank (okay, at least I knew the client's world) and the company was in a building I'd always wanted to work in and was closer to my house than the company I was working for at the time. I'd be working on strategy and consumer marketing with super creative people. And this division of the company was significantly smaller than what I was used to, which I liked (less bureaucracy).

It turns out the agency was looking for someone with my banking background, and I got the job. It was a fantastic experience. I led a big cross-functional team working with very creative and strategic people. I gained greater experience with presenting and managing clients as the agency lead for a large American corporation. Plus, the leadership at this company really had my back and set me up for success the best they could. But yes, the hours did suck, and I had not yet learned to properly manage my stress and anxiety levels.

Then in August 2020–the weirdest, most unpredictable year in my time on earth (and likely for many of you too, thanks to COVID)–I went on vacation with my family. We had rented a cottage for a week, but I didn't feel like I was on vacation. Leading up to that week off was one of the busiest, most stressful weeks I'd had in my career. There was a big client pitch happening, and I felt guilty for not being there. I had, however, stood my ground by setting a boundary and saying I wouldn't be there for it. I believe people are more productive and energized when they can truly unplug from work for an extended period of time, and I needed to unplug. I was burning out.

Halfway through my vacation, I was sitting on a chair on the dock with my two sons, Jackson and Zachary, one on my lap and one jumping in and out of the water. Next to me was a chair with my phone and a bowl of cut up apple. A gust of wind came and blew the chair into the water, along with my phone. I screamed like anyone would when their phone falls into water. My husband ran out of the cottage and immediately started wading through the seaweed (which he despises) looking for my phone (yes, he's that kind of guy). By this point I knew my phone was done, however I also felt bad for leaving an electronic in a lake. But there was no finding it.

I went inside, texted my boss from my husband's phone and let her know I would officially be offline unless an emergency came up. (There was no Wi-Fi at the cottage so my laptop was useless.) No emergencies came up. After all, I worked in advertising, not healthcare.

The next few days were glorious. I felt the most present and free I had felt in years. I didn't have this nagging feeling of constantly needing to check my phone. I could relax and enjoy our family time. And that I did.

Upon getting back to the city, it was a holiday weekend so we still had a few days of vacation left. I decided I would spend more time on my favourite hobby, writing, and went to look up what places I could pitch articles to. I'd previously written a piece about adopting our sons for Today's Parent that paid pretty well and I loved doing it. I opened my laptop (first time in over a week), clicked on Chrome and guess what popped up? An ad to become a health coach. What the heck is a health coach, I wondered. I looked into it. It was someone who helped people improve their health across all aspects, but from a lifestyle habit perspective. I was intrigued so I read on. It wasn't just a health coach program, it was also a life coaching program. It was in essence a program to help people live happier, healthier and more fulfilling lives. It sounded too good to be true. There must be a catch, I thought. I probably had to have some courses in health, science or psychology, I figured. Nope! I had struck gold.

When my husband got back from the park a couple of hours later and the kids got some screen time, I grabbed him and brought him outside to our front porch. I sat him down and pulled out my computer. In the time he was gone, I had made a business plan to a) justify the expense of going back to school, and b) show him how I would one day have my own business and make money. My husband is super conservative, especially when it comes to money, and despises being in debt. At the time, I was also making an incredible six-figure salary and was the primary breadwinner. So to now say I was going to throw it all away was a bit scary and I braced myself for my husband's spiel on how unrealistic and silly this idea was.

By the time I finished my pitch, my stomach was in knots. Then my husband completely surprised me. "This is exactly what you've been wanting to do. This is how you can help people live happier, healthier and more fulfilling lives," he said. He gave me the green light. In fact, I think he got a little bit excited too. Perhaps it was a glimmer of hope that I could work less and help out around the home more. Or maybe he sensed my excitement and that perhaps I'd found a career path that would bring me the joy and fulfillment I'd been missing and in doing so, I'd stop complaining about not having any control over my hours. Whatever was going through his mind at the time, his support showed me he believed in me and trusted that I could make it happen—and that, my friends, is really key in making any drastic change: Finding someone who believes in you at the start of any new journey can help propel you forward. If you don't already have that person, keep looking, they're out there. Whatever you do, don't let the naysayers take away your dream.

That same day I signed up for my course and a few months later I took on my first coaching clients. Nine months later I gave six weeks' notice to leave my corporate job. My dream of being an entrepreneur who helped people live happier, healthier and more fulfilling lives came true in 2021, eight years ahead of schedule.

So no, dreams (or Disney World) aren't just for kids, folks. They're for you too.

My secret, silly dreams

When I was a kid, there were two jobs that lit me up but I dismissed them because they didn't seem like actual career paths. When I say lit me up, I'm talking about two activities that put butterflies in my stomach and a grin on my face from ear to ear. Want to know what they were? Well, you'll just have to keep reading.

Here's the crazy thing, though–until writing this book, I'd never shared what my secret silly dreams were. And you know why? Because I thought they were embarrassing. They weren't something you could earn a degree for so how could they be real jobs? I come from a household where my dad was a lawyer with his own practice in a small town and my mom was a teacher. Two very specific roles with clear career paths.

Now, I'll stop for a moment to say my parents never told my siblings and I what to do with our lives, but in my mind, I needed a practical career.

So, what was this first secret, silly dream? To be a motivational speaker. Yikes, did I just admit that to all of you? It still feels a bit surreal. It all started while on an overnight trip for my high school's Student's Council. I was the Treasurer for the Council and we all got to go to a conference for a night. While there, we attended an assembly with a motivational speaker. The speaker wore a really big, silly hat like that from a Dr. Seuss book and although I can't remember what he talked about, I remember him being funny and energizing us. Not in a tacky, rah-rah way. I left that assembly feeling incredible, and that feeling has stuck with me for over 25 years.

At the time, I was a cheerleader for my high school, so pumping people up was something I loved doing, but being a one-person motivational speaker? That was freaking scary. I wanted to be someone who lifted people up and made them happier. But how the heck was that a career? I didn't even see myself doing cheerleading beyond high school. In my mind, motivating people was something you did for fun as a part-time hobby. I loved doing speeches each year in school too, and going up on the gym stage, but again I would ask myself, how was speaking a career?

As for my second silly dream job? You're looking at it right now—me writing. I've loved writing since I was a kid. The first book I started (and never finished) was about a girl named Tiffany who I think was a babysitter, likely inspired by *The Babysitter's Club*, my favourite series as a kid. And the only time I ever got called by a teacher at home was in high school after my English exam. Mr. Smallwood called me to say how great my essay was and wanted to know if I had considered taking an English degree and being a writer. While it intrigued me, I did not see it as a career. Like speaking, writing wasn't a job; it was a passion. I didn't share those exact words with Mr. Smallwood, but I did let him know that I was applying to business programs.

Silly dreams aside, I attended university to get a Bachelor of International Business Degree, which included spending my third year studying in Lima, Peru—a once in a lifetime opportunity. I loved Peru. I loved the food, the culture and all the incredibly diverse places I could travel to. I also met a Peruvian guy and went back after I graduated to work as a financial analyst for the corporate banking division of a bank so we could be together. In addition to doing my internship, I also had my first foray into entrepreneurship, when my Peruvian boyfriend and I started a jewellery business while I lived there. It turns out that it wasn't my passion, but it did give me a glimpse of what running a business could be like and I enjoyed it. My relationship didn't last, so I returned to Canada once winter had ended and I'd done some travelling to Argentina and Brazil. When in Rome, I mean Lima…

Upon coming home, I set out to find a job in Toronto and an apartment to share with a close friend. This plan led me to have one of the biggest fights I ever had with my parents. I wanted to move to Toronto even though I didn't have a job yet. I was broke because I hadn't been working, and moving to Toronto would require me to come up with first and last month's rent. So I asked my parents to loan me the money. In their minds they saw first and last months' rent plus potentially more months should I not land a job and be tied to a 12-month lease. In my mind, I saw myself getting a job in the month before the official move happened. I promised my parents I would have a job before I moved, and they reluctantly lent me the money. Sure enough, four days before my official move to the big city (and after months of applying for jobs), I landed a job at Scotiabank on the spot during an interview. Whew, that was close!

My job entailed speaking Spanish, travelling and working for the bank I had dreamt of working for when, two years prior, I had been watching the Miss Universe Pageant on TV and saw the Scotiabank logo on top of a large shiny building in Panama City. When I'd been a part-time customer service representative (or teller as I was called back then) during university, I hadn't really thought about working for them after graduating but I figured that if they had a presence in Spanish-speaking countries like Panama, they could be the perfect company to work for. The job I was hired for was only a four-month contract, but it paid really well and excited me. At the end of my contract, I was offered a full-time job with three weeks of vacation, the title of Assistant Manager and a salary bump of $13,000. It was awesome. I felt that this small town girl had finally made it in the big city. I was winning at the Game of Life.

While I'd made this particular dream come true, including going to Panama and many other incredible countries for work, something was missing. The job paid well and I was moving up the ranks pretty quickly, but it didn't light my soul on fire and if I was going to spend 90,000 hours of my life working, I wanted it to be fulfilling.

I was also keen to start a family, so next I went to work for the financial division of Loblaws where I wouldn't need to travel. From there, I got hooked on rising through the corporate ranks and making more money. But to keep moving up, I moved back to Scotiabank where there were more opportunities due to its size and the fact that I still had a strong reputation there. I hit the Director level (a title I'd wanted since entering the corporate world) but then burnt out due to all the travel and not knowing how to manage my stress. So I made one more move, this time stepping down in title to a Senior Manager, which was actually a step up in pay. I told myself this was going to be the last company I would work for. I was going to stay there until I retired.

But here's the thing: Sometimes those silly secret dreams we have come back to haunt us when we least expect it. And that haunting started when I spent those 31 days at the children's hospital with my son and realized I wasn't feeling happy, healthy or fulfilled. When I went back to work after my son recovered, I found out that I hadn't been chosen for the promotion I'd been working my butt off for. They had gone with an external candidate, someone the hiring manager had worked with at his last company. While this news stung and was a hit to my self-confidence, it was also the wake-up call I needed. I didn't envision my entire career in banking. In fact, I had done my MBA to get *out* of banking. Yet here I was, still in banking, 10 years later. Not getting that promotion was one of the best things that could have happened to me, even if it didn't feel that way at the time.

Wouldn't you know, soon after that disappointment, I received a message from my husband's former boss inviting me to a retreat at her beautiful horse farm where there would be an executive coach to help women figure out what they wanted to do for their next chapter. It was at this retreat that my dream of being an entrepreneur and helping others live better lives was born.

While I didn't see coaching as part of my dream initially, I did see speaking and writing in my future. I didn't picture exact details but I knew I wanted to be on stage and inspiring and educating people.

Both of those dreams began to happen for me after the retreat.

First, the bank I was working at chose me to lead a new initiative and as part of that, I had to present to 80 people, including the president of our division. I'd presented to groups this size before but for the first time ever, I got creative with my script and I practised my ass off. The day of the talk I was nervous as hell, but I came alive once I started talking and at the end of my presentation, the president let out a little cheer and came up to congratulate me. This moment was an all-time career high for me and cemented the fact that I loved speaking and creating my own content.

I also decided to pitch a few articles to a magazine and to my amazement, I got a response to write one with a payout of $400. I was going to make money from writing—say what?

As it turned out, my dreams weren't so silly after all. A large part of my revenue comes from speaking engagements and to date, I've spoken to dozens of audiences ranging from 50 to 500 attendees. The rush I get from being on stage is exactly how I pictured it. Oh, and I've been paid for writing a few articles with more to come. One article I published, on my take on The 5 AM Club, even landed me a radio interview with CBC, a top news outlet in Canada.

So, what secret silly dreams have you had and is it time to chase them?

Chasing happy

As I mentioned, my journey to be happier started with the stay at the hospital with my eldest, Jackson, and while I've shared a little bit about it, I want to share more of what happened so you can see why it was such a turning point in my life.

It was mid-December 2018 and Jackson had been home sick with what we thought was the stomach flu given 11 kids from his class also had it. It also happened to be performance review time at work, and I'd been anxiously awaiting to hear if I got the promotion to Director that I'd been interviewing for for months. Needless to say, I was a bit distracted. On Day 4 of Jackson feeling ill, my husband, Chris, took him to a walk-in clinic while I stayed home with our three-year-old, Zack. An hour later my husband called to tell me they were on their way to emergency to get Jackson's appendix checked. A few hours later Chris called me again, this time to tell me they were in line for surgery to get his appendix removed. I felt utterly helpless. I wanted to be at the hospital so badly, yet Zack was asleep, it was 1 a.m. and I didn't want to call anyone to come over so late. I also felt immense guilt for not getting him checked out sooner.

Upon further investigation, they realized his appendix was per-forated and his abdomen was full of fluids, making it dangerous to operate. They were afraid of nicking his bowels and causing sepsis. We didn't want to take any chances, so the alternative was to give him antibiotics through an IV for 12 days and keep him at the hospital. Twelve long days as my husband and I took turns spending the night in Jackson's room. On the 12th day, just a few days before Christmas, it was determined the antibiotics were not working and that Jackson would need surgery to have a drain put in to remove the fluids, plus a few more days in the hospital. My heart sank. We would be at the hospital for Christmas.

The day of his surgery was one of the worst as we anxiously awaited to find out what time it would begin. Jackson wasn't allowed to eat all day and yet he did it without complaining. He was a champ! Chris and I wondered if we'd both be there for it, or if one of us would have to leave to grab Zack from daycare. My parents had been staying with us and helping a ton but the day before Jackson's surgery, they'd got word that my grandma, who was 97, was on her last days so they went home to be with her and say their goodbyes. Talk about an emotional time.

The surgery ended up being scheduled for the evening so my husband had to leave before it happened. In retrospect, we should have asked someone for help so I wasn't alone. I was mourning the pending loss of my grandma, whom I was extremely close to, while I was also terrified about my son going into surgery. At the time, I had undiagnosed anticipatory anxiety, which meant I tended to focus on the worst case scenario happening. Really, it was a simple procedure that happens all the time, but my mind was going to some dark places.

The surgery took place around dinner time and as Jackson was being wheeled away, already sedated, he turned to me and said, "Mommy, just remember—be brave and always be yourself!" WTF, I thought. He was five! As touching as this was and as much as those were words I needed to hear, all I could think of was my grandma passing and how worried I was for my son. Why was he getting so philosophical? Was this a sign of something? I went to the waiting room and sat for what seemed like an eternity. Eventually, the surgeon came and found me and brought me into a room. Jackson's surgery was a success. We went home a few days later, on Christmas Day, and finally in February, it was deemed safe enough to remove his appendix.

That hospital visit changed my life and as morbid as it may sound, it was an incredibly precious time. It was the first time in many years when my career took a back seat and my sole focus was on my family.

My memories are full of doing things like wandering the halls after visiting hours, being in places we probably shouldn't have been, and watching *Jurassic Park* for the first time. I have memories of Zack coming to visit and cuddling with Jackson and holding his hand as we walked to the entertainment room, which had air hockey, a pool table and lots of games and crafts. I saw Jackson flourish, as he would go and chat up the nurses, asking them how their day was going and encouraging other patients. The less favourable memories are hearing the scary code calls in the middle of the night and praying that the child in question was OK, or when Zack asked my mom if Jackson was going to die.

We were also blessed with friends and family visiting us and sending us meals and treats. During one visit, a friend of mine, whom I'd met at a fertility clinic before my husband and I adopted our two incredible sons, told me about Michelle Obama's book *Becoming*. She thought I would find Michelle's journey with fertility and working while raising young kids relatable. I immediately texted my husband to pick it up for me on his way to the hospital that day. I found those stories my friend talked about relatable but what I found even more interesting was hearing Michelle talk about how her career didn't light her up. I was lying on the daybed in Jackson's hospital room, drinking the boot-legged wine my friend had snuck in in a Starbucks cup, reading this part when tears came to my eyes. Michelle wanted more for her career than being a lawyer. Yes, that's what she'd gone to school for, excelled at and made really good money doing, but it didn't fulfill her as much as she wanted. So, she gave herself permission to go after what did.

All of those experiences caused me to ask myself those three life-changing questions: Am I healthy? Am I happy? Do I feel fulfilled? As guilty as I felt for admitting it, the answers were no.

For so long I did things I thought I should, but let's face it, if I were a man, I wouldn't have been held to the same standards. If I were a man and wanted to change careers completely even with young kids, I'd get a pat on the back and potentially even an "Atta boy." But as a woman, I was taught to put my family's needs first. That the role of mother and wife trumps all.

Well guess what, it doesn't!

Before reading Michelle's book, I had stopped believing I could change careers. I didn't even know what that would involve. I had worked in banking since being a teller in my first year of university. I had even worked in banking on an internship in Lima, Peru. It's what I knew. But it wasn't what I loved. At least not anymore.

Hearing Michelle's story was the sign I needed that it was time to prioritize myself, my happiness and my fulfillment, and forget about the naysayers. It was the sign to get on my journey to saying a big heck yes to feeling healthy, happy and fulfilled.

Upon leaving the hospital with a healthy son (thank God), I set out on that journey and four years later, here I am. Living my dream of not only being a motivational speaker and author but also helping others to live happier, healthier and more fulfilling lives as a coach.

I get to spend more quality time with my kids during the week. My youngest now plays competitive soccer and I can go to most of his practices and games. I help out more with the kids and cooking. My husband and I spend more time together in the evenings. I've learned to better manage my stress and anxiety. I've gotten four certifications in coaching and hello, I wrote this freaking book–something I'd dreamed of doing since Grade 5.

And now it's your turn. Your turn to take that beautiful and exciting vision for your future that you pictured earlier in this section and turn it into a reality. To start chasing *your* happy. And it starts with uncovering all of the obstacles that get in your way and hold you back.

WHAT HOLDS US BACK

"There will always be three aspects of reality that will never, ever go away–pain, uncertainty and constant work."

–Dr. Phil Stutz

I watched *Stutz*, a documentary profiling psychiatrist Dr. Phil Stutz, last year and found it extremely interesting. In it, Stutz talks about how pain, uncertainty and constant work are always going to be in your life. This is an important point because it means that when you achieve the beautiful vision you pictured at the start of the book, your problems will not disappear, the hard work will not end, and you will not feel instant satisfaction. But ideally, you'll feel lighter, happier and have less regrets.

Who doesn't want to feel lighter, happier and have less regrets? I'm guessing most of you. So if that's the case, why don't more of us feel that way? Why do so many of us feel unfulfilled and disengaged at work? Why are people burning out now more than ever? Why are there several unhealthy coping mechanisms we turn to on a regular basis even when we know they're "bad" for us? Why do so many of us suffer from low self-confidence or imposter syndrome? Because chasing dreams is freaking scary. Sometimes it just seems like too much effort, sometimes we feel we don't deserve it or that it's silly, and sometimes we think things should just happen for us, without us doing the work.

Creating the life of your dreams starts with you deciding right here and now that your dreams are worth the effort. This section is a tough one. It's going to take you going deep and looking inside yourself to see all the obstacles that are blocking you from living out your dreams. You're going to have to confront your BS, fears, excuses, negative beliefs and bad habits head on and later I'll show you how to do the work to break through them. So, if you're ready to tell the obstacles that have been holding you back that it's time to get out of your damn way, let's go do the hard stuff.

It's time to call BS

To help you go after your dream life, we have to get real and by real, I mean it's time to call out your BS. If you're starting to say you don't have any, guess again. We all do.

Things like:

- I don't have any time
- I'm too tired
- I don't have any money
- People will judge me
- I'll look stupid
- I'm not qualified
- I'm not brave
- I'm not skinny enough
- I'm not pretty/handsome enough
- Work's too busy
- My family needs me
- I could lose my job
- I could lose my friends
- I could fail

Fears, excuses, negative beliefs and bad habits have different meanings, but they all boil down to the same thing–they are all obstacles that can get in the way of us going after what we want.

And many of our obstacles started forming at a very young age, when we started learning ways to either a) get out of the things we didn't want to do, or b) avoid the things we were scared of. As we got older, that list got longer and longer.

Sometimes our obstacles are legitimate, like fear of dying, but a lot of the time, and by that I really mean 95% of the time, our obstacles are just stories (or BS) we tell to protect ourselves. To not feel rejection, failure, hurt or embarrassment.

If we can address what's really behind the obstacle, we can break through it and be the master of our destiny. The truth is, we hold ourselves back for a few different reasons:

1. Because things scare the crap out of us (fears).

2. To get out of doing things we don't want to do (excuses).

3. Because we don't believe we can do it or deserve it (beliefs).

4. We prioritize other things over our goals or dreams (bad habits).

But what if we learned to reframe these fears, excuses, beliefs and habits? What if we found another way of looking at them so they weren't so daunting? So we could truly understand what's going on and overcome them? What if we called BS on ourselves and really got to the truth of the matter?

Last summer we went to a water park as a family. We have one lover of all scary rides, Jackson (age 10), and one wanna-be lover, Zachary (age 8). Zachary is super motivated to do the big rides–he talks himself into it, walks up to the top–but then fear overcomes him and he just can't go through with it. After many failed attempts to go down the Speed Racer mat slide, I asked him, "What's the worst thing that you think will happen to you on this slide?" "That my mat will fly off the ride," he said. So, I showed him that when you're lying on top of the mat, there's no way it can fly off as your body is holding it down. I never would have guessed that's what his fear was but once he was able to share it and understand that his fear wasn't likely to come true, he was able to go down the slide and spend the rest of the day having a blast on it.

Often, we don't stop and think about why we're holding ourselves back in the first place and we start to truly believe the stories we are telling ourselves.

We *believe* we don't have the time, money or energy. We *believe* we aren't smart enough. We *believe* we don't have enough experience. We *believe* we don't deserve it, we're not worthy.

Unfortunately, it's not so easy to replace those beliefs that don't serve us, because many of our beliefs started in childhood.

They're the things our moms, dad, teachers, friends, siblings and classmates said to us that stuck to our brains like crazy glue.

Like you're not smart/pretty/tall/fast enough. That you'll never make it as a musician/artist/actor so stop messing around.

But throughout this book we're going to do some exercises that will help you start to change the BS you tell yourself so it can stop holding you back.

The other F word

According to Dr. Zachary Sikora, Medical Director of Psychology and Clinical Psychologist at Northwestern Medicine, "It's important that we experience fear because it keeps us safe."

Fear keeps us safe from things like:

1. Death

2. Physical harm

3. Loss of autonomy (feeling trapped, stuck, restricted)

4. Separation, abandonment or rejection

5. Humiliation, shame or worthlessness

Fear has a huge purpose in life. It alerts us when we might be in danger so that we take precautions. But fear can also hold us back from doing things that could be extremely beneficial to us. It can prevent us from unleashing our potential. It can keep us small.

I tend to classify people into three types when it comes to fear: 1) the completely fearless, 2) those who have fears but are open to overcoming some of them, and 3) those who live in fear, where the thought of overcoming it is too overwhelming.

I'm guessing most of you are in the middle group—there are fears you are willing to overcome and there are fears you aren't. If so, this chapter is for you.

While I'm not even close to being in the first group–the completely fearless–I am obsessed with studying them. The people who climb mountains like Meru in the Himalayas, the big wave surfers who surf waves larger than 25 feet (think 5 fridges stacked on top of one another) and the extreme adventurers who hike treacherous terrain in Alaska, risking frostbite or animal attacks.

This group is so passionate about their cause or mission that they're willing to risk death to do it.

That's where I draw the line. If there is a strong chance of death, I'm definitely out.

But it also becomes my first question when I feel fear: *Will I die from doing this?*

Will I die from presenting in person with no notes to a group of strangers?

Will I die from going on that rollercoaster?

Will I die from going up and introducing myself to that person?

Will I die from putting myself out there for a promotion?

While nothing is 100% certain in life, chances are NO, I will not die from these events.

Yes, I could get super embarrassed, look stupid, be rejected, receive bad feedback, all of which suck. However, I WILL NOT DIE.

As my eldest likes to remind me when I occasionally fear sharks while swimming in the ocean–we have a greater chance of being killed by a vending machine falling on us than a shark attack.[4] Sorry, Jaws.

The great thing about fear is there is a hierarchy to it and once we know what that is and what lines we will or will not cross, it's a lot easier to face it. Remember, our fears are us envisioning the worst case happening.

If you ask your boss for a promotion, you COULD get rejected. But guess what? You could also GET that promotion, and how sweet would that be?

If you speak up in a meeting, you could look stupid. You could get reprimanded by your boss. You could repeat something that was already said when you zoned out or checked your phone. Or, you could look intelligent. You could show you're an integral part of the team. You could add value.

If you set boundaries and push back or say no to things, you could get in trouble. You could get called a bad friend or colleague. You could get let go. But on the flip side, you could improve your energy and focus. You could be more productive. You could feel happier, less burnt out.

Then there are the what ifs. WHAT IF I had asked for the promotion? What if I had gotten the promotion? Where would I be today? And you know the problem with that? No one will ever know. Ever. It's gone into the land of what ifs, only to be played out hundreds of different ways over and over again in our heads.

So, what are some legitimate fears that still suck if they happen but won't kill you?

Let's find out.

Fear of Embarrassment

I've always wondered what the secret is for those people who just don't seem to care what others think about them. Is it real? Are they faking it? Did their parents fill them up with so much confidence when they were little that they became immune to embarrassment?

I've always heard the older you get, the less you care what others think, which I believe somewhat yet I still watch people in their 70s and 80s caring what they wear and why so-and-so hasn't responded to their text or email yet or what someone said behind their back.

Perhaps caring what others think never fully disappears, but we can get better at choosing what feedback or voices we listen to.

Take a moment and imagine your most recent embarrassing moment. What comes up for you? Shame? Guilt? Stupidity? What can you take away from that moment? Next, think of someone else's embarrassing moment that you witnessed. Is it something you still laugh about with that person? Perhaps you can't think of one because most of the time we're too darn focused on our own shortcomings, we don't even notice those of others.

At age 95, my grandpa attended my cousin's baby shower (he was in great form and lived to 102). It was at my cousin's friend's house, which had a beautiful winding staircase to the second floor in the front foyer. When it was time to leave, my grandpa went up the stairs to get his and my grandma's coats. As many people were leaving at the same time, there were a lot of people hanging around the bottom of the stairs. All of a sudden, there were gasps and everyone turned and looked towards the staircase. There was my grandpa somersaulting down the stairs. He had lost his footing and somehow instead of falling straight down he had started somersaulting and did so without a scratch, bruise or broken bone. I'm sure this was an extremely embarrassing moment for him, but this moment became one of awe for my family. We still talk about it today, over a decade later, with fondness.

A lot of my embarrassing moments stem from my undergrad years and especially when I lived in Lima, Peru, for my third-year university exchange. My Spanish was pretty decent having minored in it for my first two years of university, but I knew that once I got there, people would speak a lot faster and say a ton more words than I knew so I moved in with a family in Cusco, a town close to Machu Picchu, for two weeks to take a daily intensive Spanish course. Wouldn't you know, the family I stayed with did not speak English. Amazing (said in a sarcastic voice).

I didn't understand half of what they said in the beginning, which resulted in me having freezing cold showers because I didn't know how to turn the hot water tank on. I told them I was going on a weekend trip with a couple of friends and that we were going to ride an "iron" across Lake Titicaca instead of a boat (*plancha* = iron, *lancha* = boat). I also said I was pregnant instead of embarrassed (*embarazada* means pregnant, not embarrassed), and that I had sunburnt men instead of sunburnt shoulders (*hombres* vs. *hombros*). Perhaps the most embarrassing mistake I made was when I went to the beach with my new housemates back in Lima and we ate seafood for lunch. Being from a small, largely white town, I did not have a very adventurous appetite, so when my seafood arrived in its shells and with heads still on, I mentioned I didn't like eating "*testiculos*" (which did not mean, as it turns out, "tentacles"). I'm sure my face was redder than a tomato after making that mistake.

At the time, I was mortified. But guess what? I never said the wrong words a second time! And it makes for a funny story now.

Sometimes embarrassment can bring us memorable or funny stories later on and sometimes it can help us learn things quicker than we might have otherwise. And sometimes, people are just mean and we learn the hard way who to trust and who to keep in our circle. A crappy lesson to learn but worthwhile in the end.

Fear of Rejection

We regret to inform you….

Your application to this university has not been accepted.

We've decided to go with someone else at this time.

You just don't have the experience we're looking for.

I think it's best we don't see each other anymore.

The homeowners went with another offer.

The client went in a different direction.

Your pregnancy test came back negative.

The birth mother chose another couple to adopt her baby.

These are just some of the many rejections I've received as an adult, although I'm sure if I went back in time, I could add many more.

And you know what? This list is still painful to revisit. I can still picture where I was when I received these rejections and how they made me feel. I don't remember the exact words and circumstances but definitely the feelings.

The feelings of not being good, smart, pretty or fun enough.

Heck, even my body wouldn't let me get pregnant for any knowable reason. Unexplained infertility, they called it.

I like to think of a lot of the above as *unexplained rejection.*

Will we ever truly know why we were rejected for something? A lot of it comes down to fit, and how do you explain to someone what that fit is? It tends to be something you feel.

Which is why on the one hand, getting rejected shouldn't hurt so damn much. After all, you have a pretty slim chance of getting that one job, house, partner, client. Life is a numbers game combined with a little bit of luck and the right timing.

And yet…it still hurts.

The only real way to move past it, to eventually get that right fit, is to keep going. Take action. Start racking up those rejections knowing that a yes is coming soon.

When I first started my coaching business, each rejection felt like a knife to the stomach. I took it personally. I didn't look at it as perhaps the prospect didn't need coaching, wasn't the right fit for me or really didn't have the money. On the days where I'd been up in the night with the kids or PMSing, I'd even get bitter over the rejection and go to the place of "Oh, they're going to regret their decision one day." I laugh at that thought now. Seriously, do I really believe someone is going to be kicking themselves over not working with me years later? I do believe coaching can accelerate people's desired lives, but it's not for everyone nor am I the coach for a lot of people. But what I took rejection to mean was "They don't like me."

And not being liked took me right back to grade school, when I was an outcast. Unpopular. Made fun of for my clothes, my last name (Pickell, which quickly turned into Pickle), my buck teeth, my hairy arms (which led to my nickname Hairy Pickle–ugh). In fact, I never felt like I fit in until Grade 11 when I finally found my circle. The friends I am still close with today. The friends who cheered me on and picked me up. Sometimes it just takes time and knowing what we don't want to find what we do want.

Another thing I learned about myself and rejection is it stings more when I know the person. If it's someone I don't know or a famous person, I have no problem with putting myself out there. I guess because it's such a long shot, I don't get my hopes up. And also, because they have no clue who I am, it doesn't really matter what they think of me. It's not like I'll ever be hanging out with them or in the same circle.

I have reached out to so many actors, authors, speakers, athletes, just to tell them how great they are or to ask them a question, and while most messages go unanswered, I have received some amazing responses. Take Gene Simmons, for example. Before the KISS tour in 2019, I tweeted a video of my then three-year-old Zack singing KISS songs, including him dressing up as "The Demon" for Halloween that year. No, I cannot take credit for his love of KISS–you can thank the Scooby-Doo / KISS movie for that. Next thing you know, Gene Simmons (or a member of his social team) retweeted the video and it went viral, getting over 14,000 views, with the story landing in a heavy metal blog. Zack was thrilled even if he didn't quite get it!

Then there was the time I emailed the Right Honourable Beverley McLachlin, former Chief Justice of Canada, to let her know her autobiography, *Truth Be Told*, inspired me to change my 5 AM club morning routine from how it was outlined in Robin Sharma's *The 5 AM Club* book to a routine that better suited me and is the reason why I was able to sustain it. She would wake up at 5:30 a.m. to write her autobiography, and a lightbulb clicked for me. I didn't need to follow the routine as set out in *The 5 AM Club* book–I could tweak it to work better for me. So I wrote her an email and this incredible woman, who once sat beside the late Queen Elizabeth at a dinner, wrote me back the loveliest note and made my day.

But, when it came to growing my business, it took another coach to remind me that we are going to get a lot more rejections than yes's, so what if I started counting my no's as positive signs that I was putting myself out there. After all, being scared of being rejected wasn't an option if I wanted to make it as an entrepreneur. So, why not have some fun?

To get rejections, I had to have sales conversations and to have sales conversations, I had to reach out to people and companies. And while I'm not fully immune to rejections, I know each one is bringing me closer to my dream gig or client. Then each yes becomes a bonus.

The cliché thing about rejection is it really does tend to be "It's them, not you" more often than not and unfortunately we are going to experience a lot of rejection in our lives–rejection from dating, job searching, interviewing, buying a home, trying to have kids, making friends, promotions, raises, job changes, proposals, sales. So many opportunities come down to the right time and right place with a little bit of luck, so the best thing you can do is keep going. Start chalking up those rejections as a sign that you're on the right track and doing the work. Pat yourself on the back for taking action, knowing you're getting closer to your goals and dreams every step you take.

Fear of Failure

Real talk time. How many times have you said no to an opportunity or didn't put yourself out there, because you were afraid of sucking or looking like a failure?

Gosh, I can still remember my kindergarten teacher asking me to participate in a school assembly where we sang (perhaps lip-synched) and danced to the oldies song "Lollipop." Singing and dancing were my thing–I loved them. That's all I really remember doing as a child. Putting a Mini Pops record on and singing and dancing my heart out. For my parents, my brothers, my brothers' friends. I wasn't normally shy about it. But fear stepped up that day and said "Not today, Shannon," so I said no, I didn't want to do it. And then what happened? Well, another five-year-old, Mya, was asked and said yes. And while I was happy for her (OK, sort of happy, I *was* 5), I immediately regretted not saying yes and doing it myself. Fear won that day.

The fear of failure tends to come from one of two places: a) you've never failed and are terrified of it happening, or b) failing was not an option growing up. This second group is the one whose parents wanted their kids to get top marks, excel at extracurricular activities, land a well-paying job, etc. Notice how I didn't include people who have failed in the above? Why? Because people who have failed tend to realize it's not so bad and have grown as a result. They realize failing makes them stronger, more resilient. Plus, they've done it once so now it's less scary.

Of his lightbulb invention, Thomas Edison said, "I have not failed. I've just found 10,000 ways that won't work."

Most recently, I heard some stats that blew my mind but that also make complete sense. Some of the top NBA scorers of all time also missed the most shots–Kobe Bryant, LeBron James, Kareem Abdul-Jabbar! Remember when I mentioned above that rejection is a numbers game? So is failure! As the great hockey legend Wayne Gretzky said, "You miss 100% of the shots you don't take." Failure is a necessary part of the journey to success.

In writing this section, I was thinking back over my life to the times when I've failed. I failed both of my driver's tests the first time. (Don't worry, I'd like to consider myself a great driver now.) I failed tests in my University Corporate Finance class so I dropped it. (I definitely don't regret that decision!) I didn't get numerous jobs I interviewed for, even after completing my MBA, when I thought I would be the most valuable. I didn't get speaking gigs I really wanted, and I didn't get picked by numerous birth parents when it came to adopting their babies. But the thing is, looking back, these weren't failures. They were a necessary step in the process to get to where I am now. In fact, I am leaning towards saying I've never failed because I've treated each setback, each no, each rejection, as a lesson to be learned.

The Oxford Dictionary defines failure as a *lack of success*, but if we learned something about ourselves or our journey in the process, was it truly unsuccessful?

One common thread I find with most of my clients is a fear of failure at work–a fear that keeps them from speaking up, setting boundaries or asking questions. They're afraid that if they do these things they might look stupid, get reprimanded in front of people (hello fear of embarrassment) or even be let go. And holding back can mean missing out on a promotion, getting a lower bonus, or even just watching someone else say the bright idea in your head and get the praise instead (ugh). When I first started out in my career, it was hard to be let go without your boss building a big case. Unfortunately, now that security seems to have gone out the window, which makes a fear of being fired a pretty darn legit fear with potentially devastating consequences. But you know what else that fear tells me? There are no guarantees in life. With anything! You could be let go tomorrow or you could also get a call from a recruiter for that dream job you've always wanted. Your project could bomb, you could get blamed, but on that next project you lead, you could shine as you've learned the hard way what not to do. Or, as in my case, you might miss out on the promotion you've been working your butt off for for months, but that failure could accelerate your dream of starting your own business.

In order to succeed, we have to go through the motions. We have to put ourselves in uncomfortable situations. We have to risk failure! And feedback. Ugh, feedback!

Feedback is something I used to dread. Whether it was a performance review, feedback on a document I put together or how I did in a presentation, I wanted to find a rock, hide under it and avoid the whole thing.

Why?

Because I used to anticipate the worst. (Thank you, anticipatory anxiety.)

Because the worst did happen in my very first performance review in the corporate world (or so I thought for many years). A few months in, I was having a one-on-one discussion with my boss and I thought I'd be proactive and ask him how I was doing.

He in turn asked me how I thought I was doing (gosh I hate that question). I thought I was kicking butt but downplayed it to not be boastful and said I thought I was doing well. It was only a few months into my very first job post-university, after all.

He then said, "If I had to give you a grade, I'd give you a C."

A *C*? Excuse me? I'm one of the only Spanish speakers on the team, I'm co-leading the launch of a brand new product across two countries and I'm 23 frickin' years old. A *C*? (Of course, this is what I said to myself in my head and not as questions to my boss.)

I called my dad to tell him, and he asked me if I asked my boss for feedback around *why* he gave me a C. I had chalked it up to my boss being a jerk but really, I was so devastated by his feedback that all I could do was nod or else I would have burst into tears.

I did, however go on and build a case for how much work I had done and shared it with my boss. He wasn't surprised at all, nor did he contest my accomplishments, which stumped me even further. And still, I was too scared to ask for clarity.

I ended up getting a new boss not long after that conversation, someone whom I knew well from our department. I shared this "C" comment with him as it still stumped me and I wanted him to know. He also didn't understand my previous boss's reason but assured me I was an integral part of the team and that the only thing holding me back was my age and that would change over time.

Not only did this new boss help build up my self-confidence again, but he also helped me shine even more at work and truly set me up for success.

It wasn't until years later that I realized that my first boss was going by the bank's bonus structure scale and a "C" was his way of saying the third highest rating, which was "very good," after superior (which no one really gets) and then excellent.

So sometimes what we view as "failure" is just miscommunication. Moving forward, I didn't ask a question I wasn't prepared to answer with proof myself. If I was going to ask about my performance, I would have my top three to five accomplishments in my back pocket. If I was going to ask someone how they thought a project was going, I would have the known challenges with potential solutions ready to propose. And while I still don't love asking for feedback in the chance it can blindside me like it did that very first time, feedback is what prevents us from failing at the exact same thing twice. When it's constructive, it can help build our confidence, make us feel appreciated and push us to do and be better. So don't be afraid to ask for clarification. It might be hard but it's better than analyzing a comment someone said for years afterwards.

Without overcoming my fear of failure:

I wouldn't be a mom, my absolute favourite role in life.

I wouldn't have gone for promotions and gone from a Senior Manager to a Vice-President with a $60,000 raise in salary with one move.

I wouldn't have lived in a foreign country and had the experiences of a lifetime.

I wouldn't have quit my corporate job to follow my heart, start my own business and live my purpose.

I wouldn't have gotten on stage and spoken to large audiences, something that exhilarates me.

I wouldn't have written this book.

What else might we be missing out on by not pushing through fear? Would Kareem Abdul-Jabbar be the leading NBA scorer in history if he had let his record of missed shots get to him? Would Steve Jobs have become the revolutionary tech guru he was if he'd let his first computer not selling or getting fired from Apple deter him from chasing his dreams? No! Our mindsets are a powerful thing and possibly the top thing that stands between who we are today and who we can be tomorrow. What gifts of yours is the world missing out on when you let fear of failure hold you back?

Fear of Success

I know you're probably thinking, Shannon, how is fear of success a fear? Well, because, sometimes what holds us back is that if we are successful at something, it means we must actually do the work, which can shine a light on our insecurities.

If I get a promotion, yikes, I'll have to step up and really prove to them I can do the job.

If my post goes viral, people will know my story, which feels really vulnerable and scary.

If I get this sale, I'll have to prove to my client it was worth it.

A lot of the time, success is when the hard work begins, and that can feel daunting or exhausting. So, sometimes we self-sabotage without even realizing it so we don't have to follow through.

And self-sabotaging can look like:

- Not putting in our full effort.

- Being less confident in a meeting or conversation deliberately when we know that by stepping up our confidence, it would seal the deal.

- Knowingly doing the bare minimum but then telling ourselves it was a lot of effort.

- Finding ways to procrastinate or avoid the task at hand.

- Thinking you want a promotion but never mentioning it to your boss.

Last year I had the opportunity to have a free 30-minute coaching session at a conference. When I showed up to the check-in spot, the coordinator asked me to write down one sentence on what I wanted help with from the coach.

I'm holding myself back when it comes to putting myself out there for speaking gigs with companies, I wrote.

Then I was introduced to Coach Veronique.

Coach Veronique: "Can you tell me what's going on that you want to speak about?"

Me: "I'm not putting myself out there as much as I'd like to when it comes to booking speaking gigs."

Coach: "Do you enjoy speaking?"

Me: "I absolutely love it."

Coach: "What's the worst thing that can happen by putting yourself out there?"

Me: "I get no's. No wait, I don't mind the no's. It's the ghosting I can't stand. I get ghosted. Or someone tells me they're interested, I send them all my details and never hear back from them again."

Coach: "OK, so the worst thing that can happen is you get ghosted."

Me: "Yup."

(A few more rounds of back-and-forth questions and then…)

Me: "NO, wait! By putting myself out there I could get YES's. And yes's mean I must do the work—research, prepare, practise."

Coach: "And do you not enjoy that work?"

Me: "No, I love that work! It lights me up."

Coach: "So what's really the fear then?"

Me: "That I'll deliver my presentation and suck."

Coach: "And have you had success speaking to date?"

Me: "Yes—I've gotten great reviews."

Coach: "Then what is it?"

Me: "What if they don't like me?"

Coach: "Do you think everyone will always like you?"

Me: "Nope."

Coach: "Then what does it matter?"

Mic drop!

I was holding myself back out of fear of succeeding and then eventually failing and not being liked. Ouch. It hurt a little to uncover that and see this hidden obstacle, my blind spot. But the good, and bad, thing about blind spots is that once they're revealed, they're pretty darn hard to ignore. And guess what happened next? I booked my first in-person, well-paid speaking gig, plus three more within the next eight weeks. This fear would no longer hold me back, baby!

Is being successful scary? Heck yeah! It might mean stepping out of your comfort zone. It might mean you being in the spotlight more. It might mean you practising new skills–in front of people. But guess what else it might mean? Following your dreams and feeling the sense of pride and joy that comes with it.

Fear of Loss

The fear of losing someone or something can drive us to do some pretty crazy things and act in ways we didn't really know we were capable of acting.

Fear of loss can have us throwing our boundaries out the window or accepting behaviour from others that would make our friends and parents cringe. Whether we're desperate to keep our job, friends, or that special someone in our life, understanding what lies beneath the fear is crucial to knowing our worth and how we deserve to be treated and loved.

Up until five years ago, I would have told you that my fear of loss was on par with the average person. Sure, I had moments in relationships where I didn't act the best due to jealousy and insecurity, but other than that, I didn't think I feared loss any more than normal. Whatever normal is. Whenever I worked with a new therapist and they asked if I'd experienced trauma in my life, I'd always said no.

But that wasn't true; I had experienced loss and trauma. I just didn't realize it until it came out in a therapy session, one month before Jackson's stay at the hospital. Remember I mentioned having hidden obstacles or blind spots earlier? This is another example of mine. Sometimes it takes being triggered for them to finally surface.

For me, that trigger was becoming a mom and feeling like a bad parent when my five-year-old started challenging me. He had entered a stage where he would have bursts of running around the house trying to destroy things and hitting me in the process. It seemed to come out of left field and was worse with me than my husband. We were also starting to get calls from the school about how Jackson was getting into trouble there too.

Before we adopted our sons as newborns, Chris and I had taken a mandatory three-day course called PRIDE where we learned how to parent in various situations, and it definitely came in handy at times like these. I can still picture sitting in the hallway, holding Jackson in a bear hug while he tried to hit me and having my three-year-old come out of his room and watch us with deep concern while I reassured him everyone was fine. We later found out that Jackson has autism and ADHD and we now have great support systems in place, but at the time we had no idea and were just trying to get through minute by minute.

Coincidentally, that situation triggered five-year-old Shannon.

Five-year-old me who saw my family broken apart in a bizarre and uncommon way when it was decided that my 12-year-old brother would no longer live with us and would be moving into a foster home. When my once family of five became a family of four in our house.

I always considered myself to have a better-than-average child-hood, having grown up in a middle-class family in a picturesque small town. I had loving and supportive parents; we went on incredible trips to Disney World, Hawaii, and England; and I was encouraged to go after what made me happy. I was the youngest of three kids, and my brothers who are seven and five years older than me did a great job of paving the way, so I had it way easier than they did, which helped me when I became a bit of a wild teenager. (Sorry mom and dad for the stress and anxiety I caused you in high school.) What can I say, there wasn't much to do in my town except party in fields, barns and even cemeteries. (OK, that one I feel bad about now.)

But let's get back to my real story here. My story of loss and how it impacted me as an adult.

Me thinking my childhood was all sunshine and rainbows was, in part, BS. It wasn't until I went to therapy to talk about how to help Jackson that I realized that while most of my childhood was great, there were also moments of turbulence and, essentially, trauma. The trauma we don't really talk about in my family. (Well, until writing this book, when I talked to my eldest brother to ask his permission to include this story, plus my parents and other brother as I needed some help remembering the details.)

For two years starting at age 10, my eldest brother, Bryan, and my parents clashed. Bryan was a challenging kid and he did not want to live by my parents' rules. So they argued. A lot. Eventually Bryan saw running away as his only option to not live by their rules. I don't remember a lot from those times, but I do remember their arguments and that first time he ran away. It was nighttime and we had a house full of people while a search party was underway. Bryan was found in a barn outside of town and was brought home.

But things didn't improve and a year later, when he was in Grade 7, Bryan devised a scheme to really leave town. My brother worked with his friend who knew everything about the trains in our town and developed a plan to hop on a freight train going to Montreal (about an eight-hour journey). Before school, Bryan dropped off his clothes through an opening in one train car and planned to return after school before it left the station, having memorized the train car number his friend had given him.

Luckily as Bryan was crawling into the train car later that afternoon through a small opening where he almost got stuck, a person working in a building next door saw him and called the police. As it was a small town, the police officer knew Bryan and took him home to my parents. But this was his second time running away and his safety was now in question. That night, with the Children's Aid Society, it was decided it would be best if Bryan didn't live with us anymore. He moved in with a caring foster family just outside of our town that same night. Although he clashed with them as well and had a bumpy road until he went to a school for music in Toronto at age 16, Bryan's love for playing the piano eventually helped set him on a new, brighter path.

What I remember after my brother Bryan was removed from our house is the social worker asking me if I wanted to talk about it. I don't believe I did. I was five and probably didn't really understand what was happening. I also remember having nightmares for a month straight but again, I never really put two and two together until years later. I remember gatherings being strained when Bryan and my parents were both present and them not getting along until many years later.

My mom was a primary school teacher and my dad was a prominent lawyer, and we lived in a small town where almost everyone knew each other. I'm sure they were filled with some shame. Perhaps it was easier to sweep the situation under the rug than discuss it openly. Perhaps they did try and discuss it with me at times but even if they did, since I never liked to be vulnerable in front of other people, especially my family (back then anyway), I likely shut it down. I know I didn't openly share the experience with many people for fear of judgment. This wasn't "supposed" to happen to a family, especially one like ours, I thought.

This change in my family had me starting to think that arguing can lead to people leaving. I can still picture standing in the kitchen of our first house, watching my other brother, Colin, get into an argument with my dad and thinking, Oh no, Colin is going to leave us too and then I'll really be lonely. What they were arguing about, I have no idea. It was probably over homework or going out with friends, but to me, it didn't matter. I was scared of him leaving, and no longer having siblings. I remember asking them to stop fighting and getting quite upset but never revealing why. I wasn't good at showing my emotions other than anger and it felt too vulnerable to bring up how I was feeling or what I was scared of.

Colin and I weren't that close until he left to go to university when I entered Grade 9. Looking at it now, I wonder if we kept a distance between us as a shield in case one of us also had to leave our family. Or if it was a boundary I'd put up without really realizing it. Sometimes we never find out why we did some of the things we did.

From our family's breakup, I formed the belief that being a strict parent and arguing with your child means they could leave your house forever. So, once my eldest turned 5 and his behaviour became challenging at times, I was triggered. I didn't know how to handle Jackson's behaviour. I wanted to be firm, but my fear had me questioning every move. I'd been chosen to be Jackson's mom by his birth parents and in those moments, I felt like I was letting them down. It's also not something you talk a lot about with other people unless you know they've been in a similar situation. But most of my mom friends didn't seem to be struggling like I was (or so they appeared) when we'd go on playdates. I'd have to follow Jackson around like a hawk while other moms could sit back and socialize as their kids played nicely with others. I felt on edge, constantly. And because I was a working mom hanging out with a lot of stay-at-home moms, I felt even more pressure to excel. That I had to overcompensate for having (and wanting) a demanding career.

So, after feeling helpless (and like a pretty crappy mom), I sought help. In just one session, this incredible psychologist, Michelle, pinpointed that at age 5 I had developed a belief that being strict and then fighting with your kids could mean they could leave or be taken from you. I was worried that if things continued the way they were going, Jackson might have to leave our home. I feared that I might not be a capable parent. So we started the work to transform that belief.

I left that first session, entered my house, closed the door behind me and burst into tears. My husband, immediately concerned, asked what had happened. He thought someone had died, as I rarely cry in front of him. I had not lost anyone but had just had an earth-shattering therapy session where I learned I had been living with fear of loss since I was five years old. Years of suppressing the accompanying fear and grief were released and I began to feel relief. I knew in that moment that motherhood was going to be the hardest job I'd ever do but that I was an incredible mom and up for any challenge that came my way. Shortly after this session, Jackson was admitted to the hospital for his appendix and some much-needed mom-son bonding time was had, even though it was under horrible circumstances.

Even after uncovering my childhood experience with loss and unpacking it, I still didn't recognize it as trauma until one of my closest friends shared that what I went through was in fact a traumatic experience. I had always defined trauma as having something horrible happen, like neglect, abuse or death. Canada's Centre for Addiction and Mental Health (CAMH) defines trauma as *the lasting emotional response that often results from living through a distressing event.* While my brother leaving might be a different kind of trauma from what I'd initially thought trauma was, it was still a distressing event in my life.

(On a side note, these experiences put my brother Bryan on the path of pursuing his passion for music. Today, he is an extremely talented pianist and songwriter. He's also the person in our family who probably shows the most vulnerability and authenticity. Something the rest of us continue to work on.)

So what have you endured in your life that is causing you to fear loss?

Perhaps you've been let go from your job and lost your financial stability and self-confidence. Maybe you lost a loved one whom you treasured dearly, or got your heart broken by someone you thought was the one.

All of these losses contribute to our fear. Fear of putting ourselves back out there and suffering the loss and the heartbreak all over again.

Sometimes we don't know what's really holding us back or has us scared and usually, it's not what we think. The beauty is that we have the knowledge somewhere inside us–sometimes we just need someone to dig it out.

Knowing what we're afraid of doesn't make the fear go away–if anything, it can make it more real. But without knowing what you need to overcome, how can you ever overcome it?

Excuses, excuses

I like to call excuses bullshit. Pardon my language, but seriously, think about a time in the last 24 hours when you were going to do something: Call your mom, put the garbage out, go for a run, not drink, read instead of watch TV. Now, what's the reason you give yourself about why you didn't do the thing? You were tired, too busy, not feeling well, weren't sure how to do it? Let's be real—you told yourself bullshit to make yourself feel better in the moment and to justify why you couldn't do the thing you didn't do.

But do you feel guilty now? Does the thing still have to get done and did you just prolong it? Does your body know deep down that it was a total excuse and you should have just gone for it?

We are masters of excuses. And hey, it's not our fault. Well, not completely. We learn from a very young age to try anything that will get us out of eating the brussels sprouts, raking the lawn or doing our homework.

In fact, the average American will make 2,190 excuses to validate their decisions each year.[5] That equals six excuses per day just around topics like exercise and healthy eating and skincare and sun protection. Just six? Come on, people probably made excuses for their excuses and totally underestimated the real number they tell themselves and each other every single day. I could even see it being six per hour!

Victoria Pelletier, an incredible woman I interviewed for this book, intrigued me when I saw her motto "No excuses" on LinkedIn. Victoria is a Senior Executive, a Board Director and a Keynote Speaker. I reached out to her to learn more about this motto after seeing her impressive background, which includes becoming one of the youngest Chief Operating Officers at the age of 24, a President by 35 and a CEO by age 41.

Victoria had a brutal childhood. She grew up in a violent home and cycled back and forth between her abusive mom and foster care until she was finally adopted out of the system. Victoria could have used these circumstances as excuses to hold herself back or not create a better life for herself. But instead, she adopted the mindset that if something prevents you from moving forward, it's an excuse and she wasn't going to let excuses be the reason she wasn't successful in life.

She also learned from a young age that if you want to go after your goals, you have to focus on what you can control in your life, such as your work ethic. So, Victoria focused on how she showed up at work, the hours she worked and what she delivered. She didn't have much money due to her adoptive parents' lower socio-economic bracket, but she wasn't going to let that stop her from buying the things she wanted. So at age 11, Victoria began to set lofty goals for herself that she wanted to go after, including earning her own money and getting her first job. At age 14, she became a people manager, at age 16 a manager of people managers and at 24 she was the General Manager and Chief Operating Officer for a large business-to-business services organization. While she suffered imposter syndrome from both being young and being the only woman at the table for a long time, she didn't let it stop her from dreaming big. Victoria knew that she also wanted to have children and she made that dream come true too.

Over the course of her career, Victoria realized that you can't have it all at once and that means making tough decisions. Decisions such as ending her first marriage even though it broke her heart, and choosing to leave roles and companies that weren't a cultural fit. When Victoria's daughter was two, Victoria missed a lot of big moments travelling for work. But it was a choice she made and lived with. Then, years later, when her ex-wife and the mother of her children passed away, she had to make another tough choice: move her kids from Toronto and a city they loved to New York City so she could be with them more while she worked? Or choose her family and change careers? She chose her family.

Today, Victoria's unstoppable, no excuses approach has allowed her to achieve high levels of success in her career and financial freedom to choose what she does and where she does it. Her experience, self-confidence and strength help her to stick to her boundaries and priorities so she can say no to the things that don't bring her joy.

As Victoria shares, "Where there's conviction, there's capacity." By saying no to excuses and making hard choices, Victoria was able to prioritize the things and people that mattered to her while creating an abundant, fulfilling life and career.

So what excuses are you making right now? Do you skip get-togethers after work "because I'm too tired" (aka "I'd rather stay home and watch Netflix") or do you choose to go and grow your network and professional relationships? Do you block the time off in your calendar to ensure you do your workouts or do you let the time get booked up and then say you're too busy to look after your health?

It's time to stop the excuses and own your decisions. Yes there will be hard choices to make, and with that come trade-offs and sacrifices and maybe even compromise. If something doesn't bring you professional or personal joy, maybe you could delegate or outsource it. And if it does, how can you create the capacity for the things you *do* want to do?

Calling out our excuses and overcoming them is certainly one way to start doing just that!

While none of these excuses will be new to you, let's dig in to the top excuses we use. In other words, bullshit.

Excuse 1: I don't have time

I have to know, does anyone love the beeeeep, beeeeep, beeeeep sound an alarm makes?

Pre-COVID, my alarm would sound off at 6 a.m. and I would feel like it was shouting at me. I'd hit snooze three times, just enough to make it feel like I was sleeping in but not enough to make me late.

I'd begrudgingly pull myself out of bed, groggy and sleepy from dreaming about work all night.

I'd hop in the shower, get ready and race downstairs to prep my breakfast and join my kids at the kitchen table.

Breakfast would be followed by some yelling, rushing, forgetting and grumpiness but we would all manage to pile into my husband's car at 7:30 a.m. and head to daycare. We'd make it. Through Act 1 anyway.

Then I'd have the mad rush for the bus, hoping as it weaved in and out of traffic that I would make it to my desk by 8 a.m.–a time I had designated because I thought it showed how committed I was to my job, and also so that I could have some peace and quiet to catch up on emails and work before the masses arrived.

Let's just say the motto first one in, last one out was one I followed at work for a long time. Until I made having dinner with my family a priority and then I was out of there to catch my 5:25 p.m. bus at the latest. I also believe it's better to be early than late to things. If I'm running late, my stress and anxiety kick in and out comes grumpy Shannon.

Upon arriving home each evening, I'd picture my husband and kids running towards me yelling "Welcome home!" while throwing their arms around me and asking each other how their day was. But my life is not an after school TV special and the only one who ever greeted me was our dog, Marvin. Nine times out of 10 if I asked someone how their day was, I'd get a reaction like I just told them to clean the house. Next would come dinner where Chris and I would prod the kids to eat even though "It's disgusting" and they would be full after two bites. We'd do baths, dishes, story time and get ready to embrace it all over again the next day.

Once the kids were asleep, I'd open a bottle of wine, pour a nice big glass, or two, grab a bag of chips and settle into the couch to binge watch some Netflix while trying to forget about the day. That is until I'd hear the ping of my work phone and know that I could be in for an hour or two of work responding to time-sensitive asks.

I would tell myself, I *should* drink less, eat better and exercise but really all I felt like I could do was survive. Get through the day and juggle as best I could–after all I was *too busy*, *didn't have the time* and definitely *didn't have the energy* to take care of myself.

My priorities were my kids and job, followed by my husband, friends and family. I didn't even make it on my own list and that was OK. At least that's what I believed for a very long time.

Until a work retreat where our speaker (usually my favourite part of the event) told us about an exercise where you audit how you spend the 168 hours in a week and see if it aligns with your expectations. This exercise had changed his life and little did I know, it was about to change mine too.

I took out a piece of paper and wrote down the buckets of how I spend my time: work, sleep, family, friends, TV, eating, getting ready, social media, etc.

I was sure this exercise would prove just how busy I was and how I didn't have an hour, let alone a minute, to spare.

Boy, was I wrong!

When I summed up the buckets of time, they were less than 168. And since basic math is sometimes a struggle (having your MBA doesn't mean you're good at math, as I like to point out to my husband), I recalculated it three times, each time coming short. I don't remember the specifics but I think I was short like 10-15 hours.

Hmmmmm.

OK, perhaps I wasn't being honest about my TV watching (maybe it is two to three hours a day during the week and more on weekends), so I added more time there.

I still came up short.

I didn't feel like I had free time so where was it going? Scrolling more social media than I thought perhaps, a little voice in my head said. *Ooooh, sick, burn,* as my kids would say. I added the remaining hours to social media to get me up to 168 hours, feeling a bit embarrassed that my unhealthy habits took up more of my time than I realized.

The next part of the exercise was listing how I *wanted* to be spending my 168 hours.

And since my excuse of not having time was now calling me a liar, I had no choice but to admit it: I did have enough time, and my excuses were BS. I could allocate the time to do the things I said I wanted to, that I was making excuses for: To exercise, cook and reduce my TV watching and social media scrolling.

Excuse 2: I don't have energy

You want to know what part of this book was the hardest to write? This one! And why? Because I wasn't feeling the energy every time I'd sit down to write it. Ironic, isn't it? How so much of our day or what we choose to do revolves around energy?!

Take a moment and think about when you consistently eat well, move your body or get a good night's sleep. I'm guessing it's likely when you don't have a ton of stress in your life, when things seem to be going your way or when you feel pretty content.

Now I want you to picture the last time you felt stressed and/or miserable, either personally or professionally. What did your habits look like then? Did they change at all?

I'm guessing for many of you they did and that's why this excuse is so damn tricky. Because when we feel exhausted, stressed or down, it's hard to find the energy to do the very things that may just boost our energy.

Ugh. And with 47% of adults feeling exhausted on a regular basis,[6] this is an excuse we really need to pay attention to.

Like the other excuses in this book, "I don't have energy" is a cover-up story. It's the symptom of a problem and until you get to the bottom of the problem, you're going to continue to have low energy.

One thing I wish I'd been told more was just how much energy and focus you can have when you look after yourself. I know you're probably thinking, "Duh, Shannon, we all know that." But does knowing it mean we buy into it? If we truly believed that exercising regularly, sleeping well and eating balanced meals would make us feel significantly better and would help us achieve more, wouldn't it be a more common occurrence than watching TV?

I am the classic example of someone who used to get hyped up about something–drinks the Kool-Aid, signs up for the deal, tries it for a few times and then bam, life gets in the way. Hundreds of dollars and great intentions lost down the toilet.

It wasn't until age 38 that I finally prioritized my well-being, one year after setting a goal to be healthier during our time at the hospital with Jackson. I was sick of feeling exhausted and unmotivated all the time and that a year later I still hadn't succeeded at being healthier. So,

I finally picked up a book I'd heard many of my co-workers talk about. It was time to see what *The 5 AM Club* by Robin Sharma had to offer.

A few chapters in and I was hooked. I hated the idea of waking up at 5 a.m., even 6:30 a.m. was a struggle for this sleep-craving woman—but I loved the idea of one hour to myself without any interruptions. No kids, no husband, no dog, no bosses, no text messages and no emails for one glorious hour. OK, scratch the dog part, as Marvin now gets up with me, but the rest worked out.

Basically, the concept is this: You wake up before anyone or anything can distract you and you have 60 minutes to yourself for working out, practising mindfulness and learning. Twenty minutes of each and you're set to have a more positive, energizing day.

SOLD!

And when did I decide to start this absurdly early routine? Why, in February of 2020, of course. The coldest and darkest month of the year in Canada and one month before our world got turned upside down by COVID. Fun times.

But I was excited for the "me time," so when my alarm went off at 5 a.m. that first day, I bounded down to my basement where I had my workout clothes waiting for me. I hopped on our elliptical for 20 minutes and then headed upstairs to our family room. I then meditated for 10 minutes, wrote down three things I was grateful for, listed my goals for that month and year and wrote out my 10 dreams for 2030 (more to come on this later). Then I finished by reading a personal development book for the last 20 minutes.

By the time 6 a.m. came and my youngest was up for the day, I was on fire. I now had time to be present with my family, eat breakfast together, get ready and be out the door at 7:30 to do the daycare drop-off and be at my desk for 8:15.

I felt unstoppable.

Until 2 p.m. or so, when I started to crash.

But I did it the next day and the day after that for three weeks.

Until the rumours of this illness called COVID started making its way into the daily news and the uncertainty of everything sunk in as we were told to start working from home and that our kids would be homeschooled.

Just when I needed my alone time more than ever, I abandoned it.

There was too much going on. Too much overwhelm and stress.

We picked up our kids and moved in with my parents in my childhood home, three hours from Toronto, so my mom, a retired teacher, could help our kids with their virtual school and also because they have a huge yard the kids can play in where we didn't need to watch them like hawks. Plus my dad would take half days off work and take them to a friend's farm where they could explore the grounds on a regular basis. It was great to have the help but it also meant having less and less me time as I was constantly surrounded by people.

Then in May 2020, I hit an all-time low. I was burnt out from working around the clock and I was mentally exhausted from trying to juggle it all—my kids, team, clients, meals, etc. I didn't let on I was struggling as everyone was and I didn't want to be a burden. So, I sucked it up and pretended everything was great, which it turns out, takes even more energy. I resented everyone and everything and knew something had to change. The only thing I could technically control at that time was the hour before everyone was awake and began demanding my attention and time. That hour between 5 and 6 a.m. So, I went back to my routine and gradually saw my energy, focus, productivity and patience rise—that was when I realized how important these habits were to my sanity. But, I had to change up the routine to work for me. Waking up at 5 a.m. to exercise is not motivating to me but waking up, meditating and then enjoying my coffee in peace while I journal sounds quite nice. And puts me in the right frame of mind so I can then finish with exercise.

Sometimes having strong morning routines isn't enough, though. You might be tired because your kid or dog had you up in the night and it took you a while to fall back asleep. Other times, there might be something missing from your life, causing a larger energy suck than you realize. Like with my client, Amanda.

When I first started working with Amanda, she had three goals she wanted to work on with me:

1. Make time in her day to exercise and meditate.

2. Uncover if her job was what she was truly meant to do.

3. Increase her confidence and pride in what she does so that she could be more open to accepting failure and uncertainty.

Amanda started out strong, sticking to her morning routine of exercise and meditation, where she knew that when she did it, she was a better, happier professional and mom.

But then Amanda found it harder and harder to do on certain days, so she asked me if I'd do a daily check-in with her. She figured that by being held more accountable, she would improve her follow-through. While her success rate didn't necessarily improve with me checking in, what did happen was that Amanda noticed a pattern. On the days she was dreading work, she would sleep in, and on the days where her workday was decent, she would get up. Makes sense, right? But we need to be looking for the pattern to see it. With this self-awareness, we were able to dive deeper.

The days Amanda dreaded were days where she felt a heightened sense of self-doubt and lack of confidence. She was burning tons of emotional energy stressing about work and she was feeling a lack of purpose in her job. Her work no longer gave her the joy it once did.

So we started down the path of exploring what other jobs she was passionate about, including what having her own business could look like one day, which was exciting but also comes with its own challenges. So while Amanda continued to explore her career paths, we worked on her beliefs and fears when it came to work. And guess what came out? Amanda had a fear of failing and being let go. And by working through this, she realized this fear was holding her back. She had lower job satisfaction because she wouldn't take on new roles or assignments until she was 100% ready. Sure, losing a job would suck, but it actually wasn't the money that concerned her–she was more concerned about what other people would think.

In essence, Amanda held herself back out of fear for what people would think of her if she ever failed, and that was draining the life out of her.

As it turns out, that fear is common among many of my clients, probably because I work with a ton of super successful, high-achieving individuals.

What I loved about Amanda's story is that when we turned our attention to the best case scenarios–rather than the worst case that Amanda was imagining–she realized that taking on those new roles and assignments could help her find a new passion or something she's really interested in. She could grow faster, be more well-rounded and build up more resilience to her fear of being let go.

Through our work together, Amanda was able to start reframing her beliefs and fears. Sure enough, that led to more invitations from senior executives to attend big meetings. She was even asked to facilitate a panel in front of the hundreds of people in her company. And she nailed it. Plus, she felt happier in her role and was able to start pursuing passion projects on the side that gave her purpose.

More often than not, our energy levels are linked to where we spend the most time–our work, our relationships, our home. And if we're not happy there, there's a darn good chance it's going to influence the other areas in our life and our lifestyle habits.

Excuse 3: I don't have money

A big "aha" moment for me came during my coaching training, when I learned just how freaking messed up we are when it comes to spending money, especially when it comes to spending money on ourselves for things like our mental and emotional health.

I can't even count how many transformational calls I've been on with people looking for a coach, where they've had a real breakthrough and want to work with me, and then as soon as the money comes up, they freak out and say they can't afford it.

We've all been there.

We've all said we can't afford something only to go and book a vacation, buy an expensive pair of jeans or splurge on a night out. Right? Take a moment and think back to the last time you said you couldn't afford something yet spent money shortly after on something you didn't really need and then felt guilty about afterwards.

Gosh, in my first year in the professional world, a friend of mine from Austria who I'd lived with for 10 months in Peru asked me if I wanted to meet up in NYC for a week. Could I afford it? Heck no. I was making just enough to pay my monthly rent and expenses and pay my parents back the money I owed them. But did I go? Heck yeah. I also took out a line of credit from the bank where I worked, bought some new clothes (it was NYC, after all), booked my flight and found us a place to stay for a steal.

Looking back, it was one of the best weeks of my life. Yes, I went into debt but not irresponsibly so and I had a blast. I didn't let the money hang over me all week, making me feel guilty. I knew I would pay a bit back each month, which would likely mean cutting back in other areas.

I made a conscious choice.

Now, I'm not saying to go out and rack up debt carelessly as financial stress is never fun, but I do invite you to make more conscious choices about money and call out the BS.

When it's something we really want and has an outcome that isn't so scary, we'll shell out the money, no questions asked.

My husband and I spent close to $100,000 on fertility procedures and adopting our two sons—money we had to borrow and pay back. If the money had stopped us, I wouldn't be sitting here as a mom of two incredible boys.

But when it comes to investing in something where we're not sure of what the outcomes could be? That's riskier, right?

Let's go back to the earlier example of people looking for a coach until it comes time to pay. Is it the paying that's scary? Sure, a bit. And some people just can't afford it. But, you know what's scarier? Committing to doing the hard work. Committing to stepping outside your comfort zone. Committing to change. Committing to chasing your dreams. *But if I say yes to this, I might actually live my desired life—eek!* (Nice to see you again, Fear of Success.)

The first time I went to a life coach, I remember her saying that if there was something that felt uncomfortable to bring up, that it was likely the very thing I needed to talk about. But it's also the scariest. It feels a lot like opening a can of worms.

Talking with the life coach, I discovered that the reason I was holding back on signing up with her was because I was scared of becoming a different person. Duh, that's the whole point of working with a coach—for transformational change! In my mind, I was worried that this new me wouldn't be loved by my husband anymore. That I would end up divorced. And that my friends wouldn't like the new me either. I'd be in my 40s with no husband or friends wondering why the heck I opened the can of worms in the first place.

But I was done with the toll that not being happy had taken on me so I was willing to take the risk. As I mentioned earlier, not getting that promotion to Director was the wake-up call I needed to finally pursue a career that lit me up and the timing was perfect, as it happened right after I'd vowed to be happier, healthier and more fulfilled during our time at the hospital with my son. I still wasn't sure what career path would light me up or how to go about getting it, but I knew my days of pressing the easy button and switching companies were over and that it was time to invest in some professional help.

And guess what? The return on investing in myself was 1,639%. Nope, that's not a typo. 1,639%. The amount I invested in working with an executive coach and later a life coach cost me in the thousands but the first job I got after working with these two incredible ladies landed me a $60,000 increase in base salary. Also not a typo!

Remember, this was after I lost out to an external candidate for a promotion I had been working towards for months. If I had gotten that promotion, it would have taken me years to get to that salary band.

So, how did I get such an incredible pay increase?

First, I attended that weekend retreat with an executive coach to get clarity in my career path and rebuild my confidence after losing the promotion.

Secondly, I hired a life coach to talk about how I could feel happier and more fulfilled in my life in general.

In total, I invested a few thousand dollars in coaching, and eight months later, I landed my dream job of being a VP in an advertising agency, leading a major client account with a bit of travel to the U.S. I bought my first car and felt pretty darn proud and fulfilled.

Can I contribute this ROI solely to coaching? No, but it did give me the confidence and clarity I needed to give myself permission to pursue a different career path and to share that vision with my network. Many people helped me on my journey, including past leaders and bosses, mentors, recruiters and even complete strangers who took a chance on me.

Investing in ourselves means we are investing in our dreams, so whether it's a course, hiring a trainer or a coach or buying some personal or professional development books, the ROI is usually worth it if you're willing to take action based on what you learn.

Often, as it did with me, it can lead to others investing in you too.

And you know what else happened with my transformation that was even better than the money? I got back to my authentic roots. I felt happier, healthier and more fulfilled. I had more energy and patience. I had the capacity, mental and physical, to take on more household duties. I was more fun to be around. And who wouldn't want that? I'm also more happily married now than when I started my journey, so opening that can of worms really was worth it.

Excuse 4: I'm not capable

Unlike the other excuses above—time, energy and money—the excuse of *I'm not capable* tends to be an internal excuse we may not share out loud like we do with the others. Or we may mask it with the other excuses so that others don't know what's really going on behind us not wanting to take on a bigger project, assignment, promotion or even just try something new. Sometimes it's embarrassing to admit that we don't think we can do something.

Unfortunately, this seems to be a bigger problem for women than men as research shows that men will go for a promotion when they feel 60% ready, yet women wait until they feel 100% ready.[7]

When did we stop being humans first and recognize that any change or new thing is hard and exhausting. Did you learn to ride a bike right away or did you get some bumps and scrapes and perhaps feel a bit embarrassed or frustrated along the way? These are growing pains and a necessary part of life.

Just imagine for a moment that the expectations of us were that we knew how to walk without falling, how to speak in complete sentences the first time words came out of our mouths and how to swim in the deep end our first time in the pool. That would be completely absurd. So, why is it that we expect the same of ourselves when it comes to our jobs or hobbies? And why do women feel we have to be completely ready or 100% confident before we put ourselves out there?

Because of these ridiculous expectations, so many women who get promoted or start in a new position spend the first few months practically burning out trying to prove how awesome they are to their managers and peers. In addition to landing the job they worked their butts off for, they are now hellbent on showing everyone they deserve to have the role by working extra hard. And, in doing so, the expectations for their work ethic have been set, making cutting back on their hours or effort in the future quite difficult.

Or they take the leap into their new role or activity and then immediately ask themselves, "What am I doing here? I'm not qualified. I wonder how long until they find out I'm a fraud." Otherwise known as imposter syndrome.

Telling yourself, "I'm not ready" or "I don't belong here" are other ways of using the excuse "I'm not capable." But the thing is, you ARE capable. You were chosen. You were picked. You are skilled and clever and you need to remember anything else you tell yourself is just a story, not a fact.

When I didn't get the promotion to Director, I felt embarrassed. After all, I had already been a Director at my previous company and now I couldn't get back to Director, plus I'd been filling in for the Director role while managing my Senior Manager workload. What did that say about me and my talent? I wasn't good enough. I wasn't strategic enough. I wasn't smart enough. To add insult to injury, when I went and had a coffee chat with a former boss of mine who had also recently started at the same company, she suggested I leave as not getting this promotion was like getting blacklisted. I likely wouldn't be moving up anytime soon. While this was one person's opinion and likely not accurate for a big company, I knew in my gut it was time to move on.

So, I started networking. And I started being honest about what I was looking for based on that career retreat on the beautiful horse farm I attended. Every conversation led to a new contact and a potential new opportunity. Then, one day I got an email from a recruiter to be a VP for a call centre managing client relations. I was in disbelief and figured they were just casting the net pretty freaking wide in order for me to be considered, but then I thought, what the heck do I have to lose and I applied. Well, wouldn't you know, I made it through to the second round of interviews with the president of the company. And I came in second. Sure I could have been disappointed, but that second place was the confidence boost I needed to know I *was* smart and capable and if I could come in second for a job I had never ever done before, I could potentially land another VP job.

Just a couple of months later I landed my first VP job for an industry I had never worked in: advertising. I jumped in with both feet and within my first year was recognized as an emerging leader for the company. I was also selected as one of three leaders to attend a week-long leadership retreat (which ended up being virtual, thank you COVID). I was included in leadership meetings and really felt I had a voice at the table. I was valued.

Sometimes things don't work out due to fit, culture or timing, but don't let that shake your belief of how incredible you are, because you are! And when you find the right people and company, they'll recognize you and your incredibleness.

The stories we tell ourselves

Is naming our excuses and fears enough to break out of our old habits and uncage our true selves? I wish I could say YES but I would be lying. While naming excuses and fears is huge and a vital step to getting closer to living the life you dream of, there is still one important step you must take.

Consider this step the crucial step you never knew existed but that once you discover it, there's no going back. This step is also one of the main reasons why coaches and therapists exist. To support our clients through this very important process: The process of understanding that every single comment, thought and action going back to our childhood left some sort of imprint on us, for better or worse, and formed our belief system.

When we joke that one day our kids will need therapy because of our parenting, we're not far off. All our comments and behaviours impact the people around us, and each of those people will interpret what they see and form some type of belief as a result. The challenge is, everyone's experience is unique and none of us truly understand how another person interprets what we say and do. And different people interpret the same situation differently.

If your mom saw asking for help as a sign of weakness, you likely believe you can't ask for help.

If your teachers repeatedly told you how much better you could be doing at school, you're going to believe you weren't as smart as you could or should have been.

If your dad constantly worried about what the community thought of your family, you're going to grow up believing other peoples' opinions of you are very important.

Some beliefs formed in childhood and some formed as we grew.

A great boss may have you believing you're an excellent presenter.

A boyfriend may have influenced the belief that you're beautiful.

And a good friend may have helped shape the belief that you are worthy of love and respect.

Beliefs come from our parents, teachers, society, culture, religion, friends, colleagues, and politicians. My favourite example of this is from a TED Talk I recently watched by Reshma Saujani[8], the founder of Girls Who Code, where she talks about how girls were raised to be perfect and boys to be brave. No doubt being raised to act "perfect" will influence the stories we tell ourselves and the actions we take as a result. And if we're raised that way, it makes sense that we wait to be 100% ready or qualified to apply for a new job or promotion. And men, being taught it's OK to take risks, do in fact take more risks.

The other day I spoke with an organization that is helping under-resourced youth to build confidence and leadership skills they may not get anywhere else. These youth have been labelled as "troublemakers" or "dumb" at their schools. Labels they likely now believe, unfortunately. But are they truly dumb or troublemakers, or is it that no one has ever taken the time or effort to show them the way? To support and believe in them so they can believe in themselves?

Labels are not always facts

What labels have you been given? Either as a child or an adult? What impact has it had on you?

Lia, a woman who helped me land my VP job in advertising by introducing me to the recruiter, recently shared her story with me so I could help hit this point home with all of you about how detrimental labels can be to us.

After coming back from her first maternity leave, Lia's marriage broke up and she became a working single mom basically overnight. A year after returning to work, she had a meeting with her mentor, the person appointed to her to help her grow within the company, and shared her career aspirations. She wanted to move into the consulting division of the company. You know what her mentor told her? That consulting wasn't for her. That as a single mom, she wouldn't be able to put in the required effort. And Lia believed her—until she finally realized it was not her mentor's call. Her mentor didn't get to decide where or when Lia worked. Lia did. In time she left the company and went to work for a consulting firm, and guess what? She excelled and could still be a present mom. Now Lia is married with two kids and has her own consulting business to help companies drive customer loyalty. But where would Lia be today if she still held the belief that single moms couldn't work in consulting?

Here are just some of the other beliefs I regularly hear from clients, former colleagues and friends—some of which came from feedback they received from bosses, mentors, colleagues and family.

- I'm not a good presenter

- I can't command a room

- I don't speak up enough

- I'm not as smart as my colleagues

- I don't have what it takes
- I'm not strategic or creative enough
- I'm not empathetic
- I'm a horrible parent
- I'm too old
- I'm too inexperienced
- I'm too young
- I'm not white
- I'm not a man
- My English isn't very good
- I'm not rich enough
- I don't fit in
- I'm not good enough

And here's the kicker: The person who created these beliefs in your hearts and minds likely did it out of love. Yes, love, as crazy as that might sound. Perhaps they wanted to shield you from getting hurt or protect you from failing. Perhaps they were scared to lose you so they told you things to ensure that you wouldn't leave. Or, perhaps it's the beliefs they learned growing up when their parents were doing what they thought was best. Whatever their reason, what started out as a sentence turned into a story you told yourself which turned into a fact. One that you held true. Until now. Now, my friends, it's time to confront these beliefs that no longer serve you and that hold you back.

Last year I had the pleasure of meeting Michelle, also known as Ms. Money & Math. I was looking to do an Instagram Live with a Money Coach as finance is an area I had selected for myself to work on. I was great with money when I made six figures consistently in the corporate world, but once I became an entrepreneur, my money management skills really suffered. Since I was 12 years old I had made a consistent paycheque and now I was on the hook for every single dollar I made and how often it came in. So I reached out to Michelle for advice for my followers, clients and email subscribers—and I ended up becoming her client.

I was drawn to Michelle partly due to her wisdom but also due to her story. We have a lot of similarities when it comes to climbing the corporate ladder chasing titles, designations and money. We also found ourselves questioning how to feel more fulfilled professionally when hitting the vanity milestones weren't cutting it.

In 2017, Michelle was restructured out of a job while going through a divorce. She ended up taking 14 months off, and during this time she tried doing part-time Chief Financial Officer work but found herself wanting more autonomy. At the same time, Michelle was worried about having a gap on her resume and how others would perceive her, so she went on a job search and accepted an offer. But, as Michelle shared with me, the job she accepted "was the wrong job on so many levels." It did, however, come with three silver linings: 1. She met her new romantic partner, 2. she got her own coaching certification (that her company paid for) and 3. she worked with an executive coach that the company sponsored. It was her first time working with an executive coach and as Michelle says, "It changed my life."

The coach took her on a journey of her life. It turns out, Michelle had spent most of her life in search of feeling worthy and loved. Her parents did the best they could with what they had and loved her but she didn't get the emotional support she needed growing up and sought it out in the form of achievements, thinking the more she could achieve, the more she'd feel worthy and loved. Michelle and her sister had labels growing up that also impacted her. Michelle's sister was the "pretty one" and Michelle was the "smart one." So she set high expectations for herself to constantly succeed at her career and live up to her label.

And she did. Michelle excelled at her finance career and became super successful, but deep down she knew it wasn't what she truly wanted to do. So she made a choice. A choice to go after what she felt passionate about, which was helping women become savvier and smarter investors. Michelle left the corporate world and started her own business as a money coach.

Most importantly, Michelle told herself new stories about feeling worthy and loved and what success looks like to her. Stories that don't involve hitting specific milestones, titles or achievements. She even moved from Toronto to South Africa, where she is currently living her dream and seeking her own approval above anyone else's. That worthiness and love come from within first.

The good news is, like Lia and Michelle, we can change our beliefs, stories and labels. We can choose not to let them hold us back anymore. But it starts with opening the can of worms to find and face them, and then rewrite them.

Bad habits

OK, we've covered the BS, excuses, fears and beliefs that hold us back. Now let's go to what might be your least favourite topic–bad habits. Because believe it or not, bad habits are also tools we use to keep our dreams from coming true.

How many times have you picked up this book and put it down because you weren't in the right state of mind, you got bored, or you just weren't feeling self-improvement? It's OK, I won't get offended.

I do that a lot with books too. And not just books. How many times do we have the intention to make a healthier lunch, leave work at 5 or go to bed early but something else comes up and we don't do the healthier thing? And what happens afterwards? We feel guilty for not following through or not having stronger willpower. How many times have I said I wouldn't have a glass of wine only to drink half a bottle and beat myself up for it the next day.

Does any of this sound familiar? If not, you need to put down this book and call me right now so I can learn your secrets–that or go play a game of poker because you are a good bluffer!

The surefire way to better manage anything the world throws at us is to have strong habits. I'm not saying you need to be perfect and get rid of all bad habits–gosh, there are many days where I still drink more than

I should or eat super junky food or binge-watch TV instead of exercising or putting away my laundry or writing this book. But study successful people in sports, business or Hollywood and a lot of that success comes down to being consistent with creating and sticking to healthy habits.

It starts with expectations

In order to do that, though, the first thing I want you to do is to throw out any expectations that you're *always* going to have good habits or healthy coping mechanisms with stress, anxiety, boredom, etc. Words like *always* and *perfect* should only be used in fictional context–things like fairy tales and romance novels. Picture me pressing a game show button that makes a super loud, annoying sound indicating a wrong answer every time those words pop into your mind.

Always should be reserved for things that, without fail, will happen. Things like the sun rising, time passing, and new seasons. What it shouldn't be used for are our habits or behaviours. As soon as we start getting into those areas with the word always, we're passing judgment. We're using labels. And we're setting standards, good or bad.

And *perfect*, well, that doesn't exist and by striving for it, we will constantly be disappointed.

OK, Shannon, but what do our habits have to do with unleashing our full potential? Well, think about what would happen if your house didn't have a strong foundation and a nasty windstorm came along. Would your house be at risk for damage? Of course!

Now, I want you to think of your bodies and minds the same way. When are we more susceptible to colds? When we are run down. When do you crave sugar, caffeine or alcohol most? When our emotional state is shaky or we're tired or looking for comfort.

When we are in good shape physically, mentally and emotionally, we better manage our stress and anxiety. We make healthier choices.

We sleep better (sleep deprivation is used as a torture method for a reason, y'all). We improve productivity and focus.

Through things like eating well, having seven to nine hours of quality sleep, moving our bodies, being outdoors 20 minutes a day and practising mindfulness, we strengthen our foundation and feel happier and healthier.

Habit change is freaking hard

The problem with habits is, when things are going well, healthy habits are easier to stick to. But when we're exhausted or tired, healthy habits are sometimes the first things to go. And we turn to unhealthy coping mechanisms to numb or avoid our true feelings–mechanisms such as junk food, alcohol, shopping, scrolling our phones, oversleeping, smoking and binge-watching TV. While these habits feel oh so good in the moment and are great at accomplishing our goals of feeling better, we usually feel worse afterwards, physically, emotionally and mentally.

The struggle with bad habits isn't that we don't know they're bad, it's that changing them is really freaking hard. And the proof is in the pudding. Studies show that:

- 89% of all New Years' Resolutions fail.[9]

- Americans spend about $1.3 billion on unused gym memberships each year.[10]

- More than 80% of long-term diets fail.[11]

- 90% of the online courses people sign up for don't get completed.[12]

- Over 50% of American adults don't finish one book in a year.[13]

What happens when we don't meet a goal or expectation? We beat ourselves up. We feel stressed or unhappy. We tell ourselves how shitty and incapable we are. And then we turn to those unhealthy coping mechanisms mentioned above. Or we turn into workaholics to avoid things in our personal lives.

Here are just a few reasons why habits are so hard to change:

1. We choose goals we feel we "should" achieve versus ones we really want to achieve. "Should" makes it sound like someone else is telling us to do it and who wants to be told what to do as an adult?

2. For the habits we do want to change, we don't spend enough time thinking about the benefits the new habits could bring.

3. We don't define the fears, excuses and beliefs we need to overcome in order to reach our goals or change our habits.

4. We don't set up an accountability system to help motivate us to follow through.

5. We take falling off the wagon as failure instead of looking at is as a completely normal part of the transformation process.

6. We don't address the root cause of what's causing us to fall off the wagon.

7. We don't tweak things to work better for us along the way.

Now let's dig into some of those bad habits, shall we?

Numbing our feelings

One of the topics I speak to organizations about is emotional well-being and I usually kick off with what emotional well-being is *not*. It is not feeling happy and positive all the time. Unfortunately society has us thinking we should snap out of feeling sad or that if we practise gratitude or mindfulness, we'll magically feel better. While yes, gratitude and mindfulness have proven benefits to improve our moods, there are days where we are just going to feel crappy. Period.

While numbing the pain through an unhealthy habit works in the short term, it doesn't make the pain or sadness go away. If anything, we may feel worse the next day. Most times, the best thing we can do is sit with it. Tell ourselves it's OK to feel down. That it's completely normal. And if you want to journal through it and explore it, go for it. See what comes up. Ideally, try to identify what's causing you to feel this way as we don't always know right away. Sometimes it's a bad dream that you had, or a comment someone made or a memory that popped up. And this thing may have by-passed your brain and gone right to the heart so it can take a minute to link it to the trigger. Whatever it is that has you feeling down, the only way to feel better in time is to go through it, feel it. It's like if you're dealing with a health issue that needs attention–if you try and ignore it, it will likely only get worse.

Avoiding "it"

A second bad habit we have is avoidance and this is another one of those lovely habits that may link back to your childhood. It may have been a go-to strategy for your family or your friends. Perhaps you're avoiding having an uncomfortable conversation, admitting a hard truth or doing the work to achieve your goals. Avoid it and it will go away. Wrong again. It may get buried deep inside but it will not go away.

How many of you know someone who can never just sit and relax? They need to always be doing something. Sometimes that's linked to a belief that relaxing is lazy and sometimes it's a tactic used to avoid what we don't want to face: the strained relationship with someone, your financial situation, feeling a void in your career, being lonely. If you're busy, your mind will focus on something else. But your mind won't forget and whatever you're avoiding will continue to haunt you.

Confronting "it" may bring out all the fears, excuses and beliefs you have. It may feel uncomfortable as hell but just imagine what could happen once you have dealt with it. How might that feel?

Other bad habits

Now let's take a look at some of the other bad habits we have that hold us back in life, especially when it comes to our careers. Perhaps these habits have taken the driver's seat and are steering you in the wrong direction. It's OK to admit it. These experiences helped sculpt the person you've become and were an important part of your journey. But now, it's time to acknowledge them so you can break free.

These bad habits are not having clear priorities, not setting and sticking to boundaries, not speaking up and giving in to the 3 P's–perfectionism, people-pleasing and caring too much about how we're perceived.

Not having clear priorities

During my 15+ years of leading people and teams, plus working with my coaching clients, I see two primary mistakes people make when it comes to prioritizing their to-do's and calendars. They either a) don't have them, or b) have way too many that they may as well not even have created a priorities list. Oh, and how can I forget c) they don't include themselves on their list of priorities, which means everyone else's needs and priorities tend to come before their own.

Either this is you or you know someone who falls under this category. This is the person who says yes to everything even when their plates are full and they always have a ton going on. Or sometimes this person is all over the place bouncing from one to-do to another because they're not sure what to focus on.

Why do we find it hard to have clear priorities? Usually because one of our fears is at play. Our fear is telling us that if we start saying no to things or pushing back that people won't like us as much, we'll be disappointing them, that we could get fired or not get that promotion we want.

But really, what not having clear priorities is doing is stretching us too thin and causing us to focus on too many things at once, which usually causes us to be less focused, productive and energized. Sometimes we start to resent the people we can't say no to–even though it's our responsibility, not theirs.

Not setting and sticking to boundaries

You know the famous song from the movie *Encanto*, "We don't talk about Bruno"? Well I think it's more like we don't talk about boundaries…nearly enough. I know this was a hard one for me, especially when it came to my bosses asking me to work over the weekend or on vacation or calling me when I was putting my kids to bed, and me answering (insert face slap emoji).

Boundaries are freaking hard to set and maintain and it goes hand-in-hand with why setting priorities is hard. We fear bad things will happen to us, and that our career or social lives will suffer.

Sometimes boundaries are hard because we can't say no to our bosses, clients, colleagues or family and sometimes boundaries are hard because our expectations of ourselves are too high or we're worried about what others will think. I see this with parents A LOT. Putting in the face time at the office or online so that their colleagues don't think they're not hard workers. So they "prove" they work just as hard as others whose kids are grown or their colleagues without kids–like by being a parent of young kids, or having elderly parents to look after, they're at a disadvantage. So they set the bar high and increase their chance of burnout by trying to do it all.

Not speaking up

I'll never forget the day the financial services company I was working for had a big reorganization early on in my career. My awesome direct report whom I had hired, trained and who had become a good friend was moved to a different team and I inherited two new direct reports whom I didn't know very well. After the reorg news was shared, I went and met with my new team members individually and in the first five minutes of meeting one of the women, she shared with me that she wanted a raise and wanted my help to get it. My mind went to, how could she ask me for a raise within five minutes of meeting me? I was in shock and awe. I'd never had the guts to come out and ask for what I wanted at work, at least not in such a direct way. And while I didn't go to bat for this woman right away, I did start to pay attention to her performance and quickly saw she was deserving of it.

Up until this point in my career, I had expected my work to speak for itself. And since I'd received three promotions in my first four years in the corporate world, I'd been successful with my strategy. But what I learned over time is that me getting promoted three times without asking was pretty darn lucky and more often than not, you need to speak up. While I was great at advocating for my team, it felt uncomfortable advocating for myself as my fear of rejection and failure would take over. What if I asked for a promotion or a raise and was told no, I wasn't deserving? For many years, I decided it was better not hearing I wasn't deserving than going for it.

The other reason we need to speak up is because people are NOT mind readers. And, as we'll talk more about in a bit, most people are self-ish. They're sitting around thinking about what *they* want and not necessarily sitting there thinking about what you want or how to help you get it.

I can't tell you how many times I've heard people assume that others should know they want to be promoted or considered as lead for a big project. Or they haven't done their research to understand what it takes to get a higher bonus, salary bump or promotion. One poll shows that only 50% of employees know what their managers expect from them.[14] That is a shocking statistic and shows that both managers and employees need to overcome their fears and excuses and start asking more questions.

The same goes at home too. How many of you think your partner, parents or kids should know what you want instead of you asking them for it? And how often are you disappointed when it doesn't happen?

Remember how at the start of this book I mentioned the receptionist at the foot doctor who said she could see me being Prime Minister, but how I thought politics was not for me? Well, I misled you a little bit. You see, we are all technically politicians. Not in the true sense of the definition but when it comes to self-promotion and advancing agendas, we are all politicians. And whether we like it or not, we all have to play the game at some point in our career. The game I won't play is that of deception or going behind people's backs to advance myself or my project, but there is a game to be played of promoting yourself and your initiatives.

For those of you who dislike the game and/or politics, here's another way to look at it. Let's say you're the leader of a team of 400 people. How do you know what's going on in your company? You rely on your direct reports to tell you, right? And let's say those direct reports have 100 people on their team. Can they possibly know what's going on with each person? Heck no, nor should they. They rely on their direct reports. See the pattern? So as much as you feel your work should speak for itself, unfortunately, with how big people's mandates have gotten due to budget cuts and downsizing–managing inbound emails alone is a full-time job–you are responsible for getting yourself, your team and your work recognized. And to do so, you have to reframe your belief that it's bragging. Sharing your work and accomplishments is not bragging–it's updating your manager and your team on what's going on. In other words, it's good communication!

We'll look at how to speak up and ask for what you want later on but first I want to share the rude awakening I got when I relied on others to promote me.

I was year two into my first official full-time corporate job and I was selected to go on a six-day course to Atlanta, Georgia, to learn about all things credit cards. I had travelled somewhat for work up to this point but had yet to attend a course. For someone who loves personal and professional development, I felt like I'd won the lottery. It was the perfect mix of learning and fun (perhaps even too much fun at times).

Back then I was still under the assumption that when you attend a conference or course you had to attend every single event that was put on. (I quickly learned to tailor my schedule to what interested me as I matured.) I was asked to take notes so I could share my learnings with the team when I got back. I had pages and pages of notes I couldn't wait to share.

I returned to work feeling energized, more confident about my industry and had grown my network of contacts to stay in touch with. Two days after returning back to the office, in our weekly departmental meeting, my colleague who was the only other person from our company who had attended the course with me stood up and presented her learnings from the course. She had put a lot of effort into her slides and notes, and I had no clue she was going to do it. She didn't even mention I had also attended. I was blindsided.

Afterwards, my boss pulled me aside, clearly blindsided as well and annoyed. He asked me why I wasn't a part of the presentation. My opportunity to shine was gone, which not only impacted me but also my boss who had campaigned for me to attend this costly course. I can still remember the pit in my stomach and how hurt I felt that this colleague would do that to me. (That's the part of the game I dislike and won't do to others.)

It was a necessary lesson, however, and although I won't play a dirty game, I did realize I would need to start playing the game like a pro. From that time forward, I would be the first to share learnings (and include my peers), give thanks for opportunities and shine!

The 3 P's-perfectionism, people-pleasing and perception

Do any of the above bad habits ring a bell for you? If yes, you are not alone. So many of the people I've led and coached struggle with at least one of these habits. Why do we struggle with these habits? Because of the 3 P's. The 3 P's that hold us back in our careers and kill our potential: Perfectionism, people-pleasing and perception slow us down and rob us of opportunities. The opportunity to launch something or speak up before someone else does. The opportunity to prioritize our desires. Perfectionism, people-pleasing and worrying about perception help make people decent human beings and are great for certain situations and roles but once they start interfering with your goals and dreams, they need to be dialed back.

Striving for perfection

Ok so there are a few scenarios where aiming for perfection is important–health care, construction, transportation. Things that can literally impact life or death. But as for the rest, striving for perfection can be a vicious cycle. In fact, depression, anxiety, eating disorders and other mental health problems can come from perfectionism.

For those who rank high on this habit, I'm guessing that perfectionism trait started when you were a child. Perhaps your parents were perfectionists or had high standards for you. Or you were in competitive sports, or excelled at school, and you set the bar high for yourself from a young age. I'm guessing many of you are super high achievers and therefore continue to set the bar high for yourself and perhaps the others in your life.

Gosh I can't even count how many times I would be upset with something at work and my husband would have to remind me that a lot of people don't have such high expectations as I do. In fact, I don't even think I'd ever really considered that until he mentioned it to me. I set my bar really high, and I just assumed everyone else did too. That was a hard lesson for me as a leader as it means you can't hold everyone to the same standards you hold for yourself or you'll end up feeling constant disappointment, which isn't really fair to them or you. The same goes for our kids, partners, friends, family and the expectations we have of them.

Just last week I asked one of my fabulous clients what her definition of success is for the next 12 months. You know what she said? "To know everything and everyone for the area of the industry I work." She then added a few more items. When she was done, I repeated back what she'd shared and I waited to see what would happen when I got to that line. Her eyes widened and she jumped in and said, "Well that's ridiculous to think I can do that." And she was right–she was setting an impossible goal for herself–one that would have seen her fail. So, we tweaked the definition to be more realistic and less "perfect."

Instead of aiming for perfection–come on, we all know that's humanly impossible–how about we strive for whatever our definition of *great* is and what works for us in our lives at that point in time. If you have little kids at home and aren't getting much sleep or you're not able to have any "me time," you may not be doing your absolute best at work. And guess what? That's OK! You're allowed to stop giving 110% to everything you do and dial it back so that you don't burn out. You're allowed to prioritize family and friend time over work and still be successful. You're allowed to have different periods of different motivators and drivers in your life. It doesn't mean it will stay that way forever. It just means that this is what works best for you in this moment.

People-pleasing

If you're already thinking, "Oh no, if I don't give 110% at work all the time, I'll let my boss down," then your inner people-pleaser is right on time. Hello there, people-pleaser, nice to meet you. I like to think of people-pleasing as putting everyone else's needs before your own. You're willing to set aside your work to help other people with theirs even if it means you're now working at night or on the weekend to catch up. It means you don't like saying no because you don't want to let anyone down. What's ironic is that often you're helping someone else out when most likely *you're* the one who could use the help. The thing about people-pleasers is that they're lovely people because they always say yes. But who does a boss or friend go to when they need help? The one who they know will say yes (rejection sucks, remember), so once you become that person, it's really hard to shake it. It's like those actors who get typecast as a certain role and can never get out of it.

By saying yes to an ask, what do you have to say no to? If you're now working on the evenings or weekends, what are you missing out on? By agreeing to do all of the baking for your kids' school's bake sale, what are you giving up? Or by always being the note taker, the one to clean up after a lunch and learn, or the person always making the dinner reservations for your friends, what label are you giving yourself and is that how you want to be perceived?

Isn't it time to start saying yes to yourself more so you can have more of what *you* want in your life?

Perception-caring too much about what others think of you

Why the F does it matter so much what others think? Why can't we just flip a switch and turn that part of us off? (Well not completely off, as we'd likely all turn into assholes, but dimmed just enough so that we don't hold back out of fear of how we'll be judged.) Because many of us from a young age were taught that other peoples' opinions of us matter and we should watch how we act or what we say so that we don't come off a certain way.

Then as we get older, we watch what we say or do out of fear.

Fear of being judged.

Fear of not being liked.

Fear of not belonging.

Fear of being let go.

Fear of not getting a promotion or a raise.

Fear of getting it wrong.

Fear of letting someone down.

Fear of looking different.

Fear of being laughed at.

Fear of not being good enough.

These are just some of the fears that go through our heads on repeat, especially in uncomfortable or anxiety-driven situations. Situations like being in a meeting with senior leaders, presenting to a large audience, wanting to share your opinion, picking out your clothes for a night out, hanging out with a new group of people. Did you know that we have an estimated 60,000 thoughts a day[15], 80% of which are negative and 95% that are exactly the same as the day before?[16] That's a lot of beating ourselves up every day.

I also want to point out that while you're sitting there worried about what others think of you, others are sitting there thinking about themselves. People are selfish. We think of ourselves way more than other people think about us. Truly, other people don't think about us as often as we think they do.

If you don't believe me, test it out. Start noticing how often your thoughts drift to yourself in a day. These can be positive or negative thoughts. Perhaps you're judging a parent and thinking to yourself, you would never have handled that situation that way. Perhaps you're looking at your leader and thinking of what qualities you admire and want to start working into your style. Or maybe you like someone's graphics in their presentation and you're telling yourself you need to up your PowerPoint game. Or when someone tells a story, how often does it trigger you telling a story that is similar? See how our perception of others always circles back to ourselves?

No one will ever remember as much about what you said or did as you will. We're not going home and reanalyzing all the lines someone said in a conversation unless it was stuff about us. We don't critique everyone's presentation line by line. Sure, we may have thoughts and judgments of others from time to time–we're human, after all–but on any given day, chances are you're thinking about yourself *way* more than anyone else.

These are completely normal things we all do but it's when we hold ourselves back or pretend to be someone we're not because of perception that we're doing a disservice to ourselves. The not speaking up in a meeting or asking that great question during a presentation, not asking a new friend to go for a coffee, not raising your hand to lead a cool project.

In my case, I didn't get my first tattoo until I left the corporate world because for years I thought it would be seen as inappropriate or hold me back from rising the ranks. Now, I have a beautiful tattoo on the inside of my right wrist of birds in flight reminding me to break free, chase my happy and freedom, and stop caring so goddamn much about what others think!

Not only is trying to be someone you're not exhausting, but it's also keeping the world from all your incredible gifts. When you're not afraid to be yourself, more people will like you because your true personality will shine.

Only you can make the change

All of the above bad habits are linked to fears or negative beliefs we have which are legit and scary and make us feel super crappy when they happen, but part of wanting to be bolder and setting yourself free involves taking risks. It involves being in the spotlight for more critics to judge you. Yes, your feelings could get hurt and your ego may take a hit, but when you're near the end of your life, what would make you more content? Knowing you drove your own damn car and gave it your best or that you sat back and let someone else take the wheel, so you didn't get hurt (physically or emotionally)? The choice is yours and only you can make it. Whatever you choose is great, as long as you can live with your decision.

When I started my last corporate job, I decided to show up more authentically, which I did. But I was also working in the advertising industry, where we produced marketing for clients and where the 3 P's can play a big role. After all, if your clients aren't happy with your work, you risk losing them and millions of dollars of revenue. And if that happens, well you can lose your job. But sometimes that fear of job loss plays a bigger role than we realize. And it can get in your head and cause you to second guess your work. You want to strive for perfection but sometimes don't have the time. Or your clients weren't clear with their ask, but you fear asking them to provide more details in case they get offended or mad. So you lean into people-pleasing and caring what they think.

As I mentioned earlier, the 3 P's can be great–to a degree–but they can also cause us to spiral, doubt ourselves and our abilities and be less decisive.

I was headed down that slippery, dark path *until* I made my decision to go back to school and strive towards following my dream of being an entrepreneur. Once I started doing my coaching certification on the side, it also provided me with a back-up plan. I knew I'd be leaving in a year's time and while I didn't want to burn bridges, the fear of losing my job no longer ruled me. I felt free. I'll never forget the day my boss told me that when I came back from that week's vacation (the one where I decided to chase my dreams after my phone fell in the lake), that she saw a shift in me. I came back more confident and outspoken. And she loved it! Needless to say she didn't know the whole story but isn't it interesting what can happen when fear no longer rules how we act?

When you reduce your desire to be a perfectionist people-pleaser who cares about others' perceptions of you, you can implement strong, healthy habits. Habits such as knowing your priorities, setting and sticking to boundaries and speaking up. And once you're doing those, you'll have the energy and drive to finally set yourself free and focus on living the life you want, not the life you think you *should* live.

Exercise: What Holds You Back–Facing Your Obstacles

For this exercise, I invite you to be as honest and vulnerable as you can. Write down the answers to the following questions as though no one will ever read them. Because, guess what? No one but you needs to know what's really standing in the way of your dreams.

You're going to take some paper or one of your devices and you're going to write the title My Obstacles. Then, you're going to make a list for each number below.

1. The BS list: When you think about going after what lights you up, what are all the reasons that come to mind as to why your dreams are silly, unrealistic, irresponsible or stupid. Write them all down–without judgment. Just get them out of your head and onto a piece of paper.

2. The fears list: What fears do you have when it comes to chasing your dreams? Are there uncomfortable conversations you need to have? Are there money concerns? If you don't succeed at first (which is highly likely), what fears come up with that?

Do you fear you don't have the right skills or experience? What fears do you have when it comes to the relationships in your life? Do you fear success and if so, what is it about success that scares you? Write all of your fears down, big and small.

3. The excuses list: You guessed it, it's time to get all of your excuses on the table and by table I mean piece of paper. What are your go-to's when it comes to doing something you don't want to do? Or if something scares you? What are all those excuses you use on a daily basis! Get them all down.

4. The negative beliefs list: This list may repeat some of the items above and that's OK. What this list is doing is highlighting the beliefs, or rather stories, you've ever told yourself about living your desired life. Perhaps you feel like you don't deserve it or feel guilty for wanting more. Perhaps you feel like you're not good enough and that's what's held you back in life. Or that you're not smart enough or strong enough. Now is your time to write those things down and feel the feelings that go with them. If it feels painful or sad, that's a sign of something that could have been impacting you perhaps more than you know.

5. The pesky habits: Although I didn't really go into them, what are the pesky personal habits you have that might not have you operating at your best? You know, the ones related to sleeping, eating, exercising? What habits need to be kicked to the curb or tweaked? When you're stressed or tired or feeling down, what unhealthy coping mechanisms do you turn to? What things or feelings are you numbing or avoiding? What 3 P's are impacting you the most? Let's get all your pesky habits down on paper.

Now, let's all stop and take some nice deep breaths in and out and relish the fact that you just did some really hard stuff. You just dug deep and uncovered the obstacles on your path. You faced your BS, fears, excuses, negative beliefs and bad habits that are holding you back and keeping you from your dreams. And while it may still feel heavy that you went there (that's completely normal), it was a crucial step on your journey and you, my friend, are now ready to take the next step: setting yourself free.

WHAT SETS US FREE

"Whatever you think you can do or believe you can do, begin it. Action has magic, grace, and power in it."

- Johann Wolfgang von Goethe

Whether you know it or not, you've got courage! Just choosing to read this book to learn to free your true self on the world is a big step. It means you want to face your obstacles and break through them. So, kudos to you for getting this far. It's not easy and–here's one thing you're not going to like hearing–it's about to get even messier. Chances are you're going to feel worse before you feel better. But the good news is, once you're feeling that uncomfortable, crappy feeling, you are on your way to transformation. It's a sign you're moving in the right direction, trust me. So stick with it, and it will be oh so worth it.

This section is all about taking action. After all, that's what separates those who are successful from those who aren't–they make an effort, they put themselves out there, they get uncomfortable. Growth doesn't happen when we're comfortable–it happens when we're learning. So now that you know the obstacles standing between you and that beautiful vision you pictured at the start of the book, it's time to make it happen—but how to make the never-happened-yet take place?

With the steps and tools provided in the following chapters. Some of the exercises to follow will feel exciting, some will help transform your mindset and others will challenge you to put yourself out there and do the things that scare you. And some are to help you form healthier habits to give you the energy to go after your dreams, especially for any of you feeling burnt out right now. Because the only way to truly overcome our BS, fears, excuses, beliefs and bad habits that are standing in the way of our dreams is by confronting them and taking action. Plus, you'll hear some success stories from other inspiring women who overcame the obstacles on their path and turned their dreams into reality. Now, it's time to get you closer to that beautiful vision you have.

Let loose and dream, baby

Remember all the excuses, fears, fake stories and bad habits you iden-tified earlier? These are the obstacles on your path and now is the time you need to choose—are they going to cause you to stop and turn around or are you going to call out your BS and push forward? It is this choice that will determine your future. Is it scary as hell? You bet it is. If it was easy to get what we wanted in life, my job or this book wouldn't exist and we'd all be walking around a heck of a lot happier.

That's why vision is so important. Without a strong and motivating vision, what holds us back will continue to win. Those fears, excuses, fake stories and bad habits will continue to have you believing you don't deserve better. That you deserve to play small. But you are worthy of whatever lights you up.

Now, let's put it into practice.

I want you to load up that beautiful vision of your desired life once more. The vision you have before self-doubt and guilt creep in. The vision that gets you giddy with excitement. Remember, it doesn't have to make sense. You don't have to be qualified for it. You do not need to know *how* it will come true, BUT—and this is a big but—you do have to *believe* in it. I want you to keep this vision close as you go through this section as that is the reason the work is worth the effort. I want that vision to excite you so damn much that you are willing to get uncomfortable and grow like you've never grown before. That vision is what is going to get you through the hard stuff.

Can you take a moment, close your eyes and envision this crazy exciting future you want and let that smile form across your face? Let those butterflies flap in your stomach and let your heart grow warmer with hope.

What's the reason you picked up this book in the first place–who do you dream of becoming when you can throw out the how and the when? What does your life look like in five or 10 years? How does it feel? What excites you about that? What opportunities will that bring that you don't have today? Who else will benefit?

Your vision is exciting. It's motivating. It deserves a jump into the air with heels clicking. And my friend, it is closer and more attainable than you think.

Remember at the start of the book, I shared that in 2020 I started writing down my 10 daily dreams for what I saw in my life for 2030, an exercise I learned from Rachel Hollis in *Girl, Stop Apologizing*?

Here are a few of those dreams I wrote down, the ones that have come true or continue to be a work in progress:

- I am a successful entrepreneur who helps others live happier, healthier, and more fulfilling dreams.

- Chris and I have an exceptional marriage.

- Our boys are kind, funny, smart, happy, healthy and authentic and pursue their passions.

- I have a strong, loving, open relationship with my sons.

- I am happy, healthy and fulfilled.

At the time I wrote these goals, I had no clue how the first and last ones would happen. I just knew that I wanted them and I had 10 years to figure it out. But, by putting focus on my dreams, opportunities started to present themselves to me that I may not have seen before. Opportunities like becoming a health and life coach through an online ad. Or the opportunity to go on a mother-son trip to Yellowstone National Park that I may have previously said no to because I thought it was too expensive but which was the perfect opportunity to unplug and bond with my eldest son, creating lasting memories. Vision, and focusing on the what, not the how, got me there.

Exercise: The 10 Feels

I've taken that 10 dreams exercise, given it my own twist and now we're going to take it for a spin: We're going to do *The 10 Feels*. After all, a dream isn't a dream if it doesn't evoke feelings of hope, joy, pleasure or excitement. So while you're still going to write down your 10 dreams, the top criteria is that they evoke feelings that make you smile.

But we're also going to get morbid for a moment as we do this. I want you to picture lying on your death bed (hopefully at a very old age after a life well-lived) and I want you to think of 10 things that you could look back on over your life and think, Wow, I really knew how to live, laugh and love. What would those 10 things be that would make you feel proud?

Now, I want you to write these 10 things down. Don't worry about the timeline or the how. (Picture an older man from Brooklyn, NY, telling you to "just *fogget* about it.") Drop the guilt or caring what others think. Just write.

A couple of things before you get started:

- Write about your 10 Feels as if they were a done deal.

- Paint a picture with your words—describe the dream in detail so you can really picture and feel each item.

Here are some thought-starters to get you going:

- What do you want in your life relationship-wise? If you're in one now, how do you want it to be and feel in the future? If you're not in one, what would an ideal one look like? What traits are important to you?

- What could your career look like? Don't get bogged down in titles or industry but rather the types of activities you do. What's the culture of your work like? Your colleagues? Where do you work? What ignites your passion?

- What activities do you picture being important in your life? Perhaps you have a hobby that brings you joy? In my case it's "We travel the world and see awe-inspiring sights."

- Where do you live? Do you have a vacation home? What does the setting look like?

- Money, money, money. What's important to you about money? Do you picture making a certain amount? Write it down. If you're being conservative, add a zero to it! Do you have debt you've paid off? Have you bought something like a cottage, boat, new bicycle? Write it down. Describe it.

- Who's in your life? What qualities do they have that are important to you? How do these people make you feel?

- What legacy are you working on leaving? Are you a contributor to your community and if so, how? What might that look like? What causes are important to you? What impact do you want to have? Again, you don't need to know the specifics of what this is, but describe what it could look like.

- Are you raising kids or pets? What's important about that to you? If kids, what qualities do you strive to teach or influence them to have? If pets, what kinds do you have and how many?

- What else is important to you? Perhaps family time, social time, and having a good work-life balance (whatever that means to you)?

- Do you dream of accomplishing any big goals? Running a marathon? Writing a book? Winning an award in your industry? Performing in a play? Write it down, no matter how big or crazy it seems right now. You have time to figure it out.

Now that you've got your list, I want you to spend the next week writing these 10 Feels down every day and see how they–you guessed it–feel. Are they inspiring? Are some of them too conversative because you're scared someone might read them? If that's the case, too f'n bad–these are your dreams and I want you to go BIG. So, scrap the conservative ones and write the scary, audacious ones down. I want you to feel uncomfortable with these–dreams are meant to seem slightly unattainable. That's half the fun.

One of my dreams includes my ideal monthly income and guess what I was told to do by a coach the first time I wrote it down? Add a zero to it. Say what? Adding a zero to it makes it pretty crazy but it also excites me a heck of a lot more than the number I had in there. So, I did it and that is the number I now write down daily.

Once your list feels good, you're going to write it out every single day. Yes. Every. Single. Day. Why? Because you are feeding your subconscious. And what does that do? It helps you to manifest them. There is a belief that what you put out into the universe can come back to you, also known as the law of attraction. So put it out there, let it excite you and see what opportunities come your way.

Exercise: Bringing Your Vision to Life

The next exercise I invite you to complete is to create a vision board. A vision board can be done physically or electronically but I encourage you to pick what you gravitate to more. In my case, I did a digital vision board on Canva and while it looked pretty, it just wasn't as inspiring to me as cutting out pieces of a magazine or printing things off and gluing them onto bristol board. But I am a child of the 1980s and '90s so if you're younger, digital may be more your thing and that's awesome!

Also, if money is an issue, I encourage you to leverage the Internet instead of magazines as holy crap, they are expensive!

When it comes to making a **vision board**, here are some general guidelines but remember, the key to this (and every other piece of advice in this book) is to make it yours! Do what works for you as that will always be more motivating than trying to convince yourself something will work.

1. Choose words, pictures and quotes that evoke the feelings you got when you envisioned your life in 10 years.

2. Be aspirational–it's OK if you're a bit embarrassed or feel silly for putting something on your board. If you love it and it evokes a positive feeling, use it!

3. Try and find something that represents each one of your 10 Feels.

4. Include pictures or quotes of your idols.

5. Include words of what's important to you or how you want to feel.

6. Pretend no one is ever going to see it but you.

7. Have fun with it!

Then, when it's done, put it in a place you can see it or at least have handy if having it on display feels too vulnerable or embarrassing. Ideally, you want to look at it every day after you've written out your 10 Feels. And on those days you feel like you're moving backwards or that your obstacles are getting bigger, take that vision board and look at it–remind yourself why you're working hard to make it happen. Envision accomplishing these 10 Feels and believe in it, baby!

Cementing the belief

What you believe influences you more than you realize. For example, my eight-year-old plays competitive soccer and if he knows he's playing a good team, he sometimes states his team is going to lose. As you can imagine, I'm all over that one–if you think you're going to lose, guess what? You're probably not going to give it your all or you might play with less confidence. The reverse can happen too. If you are overly confident, you may not make as much of an effort either and can end up losing. The idea is to be confident but still give it your all.

If you're skeptical, that is A-OK. It's hard to believe in things that aren't backed 100% by science or that you can't touch or see. I get it. And hey, my husband is one of these skeptics and I don't hold it against him. I, on the other hand, have seen it work more than once for myself and so I believe. Remember how in 2020 I wrote down I was a successful entrepreneur who helped people live happier, healthier and more fulfilling lives but I had no clue as to how I could ever make that come true? It came true less than two years later and continues to ring true with the hundreds of individuals I've helped through my coaching and speaking. And it's a big reason why I'm writing this book.

In 1990, Jim Carrey wrote himself a check for $10 million dollars for "acting services rendered" and dated it five years into the future on Thanksgiving. He was not yet known at the time and was broke. He kept the cheque in his wallet, even though it got ratty and torn over the years. Then, right before Thanksgiving in 1995, he was told he would make $10 million for Dumb and Dumber. Carrey worked his butt off to get that part but was motivated by his belief in making the $10 million dollars.

Another story I love comes from actress Viola Davis. (If you haven't yet read or listened to her memoir, *Finding Me*, I highly recommend it.) Viola's manifestation came about in the form of praying to God. She was single and wanted to find someone to spend her life with. Her friend told her to pray to God and list all of the qualities she was looking for in a man. So, she did.

She got down on her hands and knees and said, "I want a big black man from the South who's probably been married before. Has kids, because I don't want any pressure in that department." She continued to list other qualities such as potentially being an actor and religious.

Someone whose values aligned with hers. And just three and a half weeks later, she met Julius. An ex-football player, previously married, dad of two kids and an actor himself. Plus he was a church-goer.

In my case, in addition to manifesting being an entrepreneur who helps people, I unknowingly manifested two other things. The first one was living near the water. I'd always dreamt of it having grown up on one of the great lakes in Canada. But, growing up near water in a small town is very different from a big city. Living near the water in a city is damn expensive. But, it's what I envisioned if I was going to live in the city and that vision came true. I now live a 30 second walk to a beach and can see a smidge of the lake through my second storey windows. The other example is becoming a motivational speaker. I seriously thought that was a ridiculous dream yet here I am educating and influencing audiences of all sizes on how to live happier, healthier and more fulfilling lives.

Don't just believe, do

The problem with manifestation is that there are people out there who believe that just by sitting around and wishing for something to happen, it will. I'm sure there are cases where this did happen, people winning the lottery or hitting it big at the casino. That is pure luck and not what we are talking about here. What makes manifestation work is when people believe their actions will be rewarded and take the action they may not have taken otherwise. When the belief pushes you to step outside your comfort zone and overcome your fears. Because remember, without action you can't achieve your goals. Your beliefs fuel your thoughts which fuel your actions which fuel your results.

Beliefs → Thoughts → Actions → Results

Repetition fuels belief, for good and bad! Negative beliefs fuel negative thoughts, which can lead to unhealthy habits and cause unfavourable results.

You need to believe in your goals and dreams, tell yourself things *will* work out but then, most importantly, you need to take steps towards those goals and dreams, even if they're small to start. Because without action, there are no results. It would be like riding a bike without ever learning how to balance on one–you can believe in yourself all you want but if you don't get the balance down by practising, you'll never be able to ride the bike.

So, what do you say, ready to give it a shot? You never know what might happen.

Load up that glorious vision of phenomenal future you one more time, and keep the vision close for your journey. If you're feeling it, why not stand up and do a little dance or celebration that you are on your way. Sure, it might feel silly but if the journey doesn't have some fun and silliness along the way, then what's the point?

Drive your own damn car

Buckle up, dear readers, it's time for you to sit in the driver's seat and take responsibility for that beautiful vision and your life. No one else is going to get you to where you are going but you. No one else cares as much as you do about your dreams. And at the end of the day, no one owes you anything. It's all up to YOU!

Harsh? Perhaps, but until you realize you are the only person in control of your life, you won't fully commit to taking the steps required to create and live the life of your dreams.

The first step towards creating any change in our lives is first having an awareness of the behaviours that need changing. (Remember the list you made in *What Holds Us Back?*) Although it sounds simple, having awareness can be quite tricky. Why? Because so many of our habits lie in our subconscious. We don't even know we're doing them. That's also why so many people, especially athletes, have coaches. Coaches are trained to notice these things and point them out in a nonjudgmental way.

For example, how many of you had a shower today? How challenging was it to get in, wash your hair and body, perhaps shave and then get out and dry off? I'm guessing you barely remember it as it's become such a regular habit in your life. But do you ever have those days where you do one step differently in the shower and then it throws you right off? Or how about the days you start thinking about something else and next thing you know you're washing your hair twice because you can't remember if you did it already or not? I call this autopilot. For so many tasks in our lives, we are on autopilot. Autopilot is fabulous for many habits, such as getting ready in the morning, but it can be a real pain when we want to stop certain habits.

So, we have to learn to call ourselves out. And we have to be brutally honest. Remember how often we justify our actions to get out of doing something? I want the complete opposite here. I want you to be like, "Hey Shannon, I saw what you did there. You said you were tired to get out of exercising but damn girl, you are fooling yourself. You know exercise would give you energy–you just don't feel like getting off the couch right now."

Or perhaps you're looking for a new job. You're on LinkedIn and you're looking at job descriptions and one line stands out. *Must have 10+ years of experience.* You only have nine so you immediately tell yourself, nope that's not the job for me, I'm not qualified. This is the habit of giving yourself an out because it is easier than doing the work to apply for the job. Well, I call bullshit! Maybe you don't have the exact qualifications on the list. But really, who does? So often now companies are looking for fit over skills, so why not go for it? If it comes down to you and one other candidate and the only difference is that the other candidate has one more year of experience, so be it. The right job is coming for you soon, but how will you know if you disqualify yourself first? Your job is not to disqualify yourself–that's the hiring manager's role. Your job is to put your best foot forward, and the right job will come along!

One of my favourite client stories is Rachel's. Rachel was super skeptical about working with a coach but was working on changing jobs and wanted to start that next job strong and with increased confidence. By the time Rachel and I kicked off her program, she had already landed her next job in the area she wanted to move into and for a boss she really clicked with. Things were off to a great start. Then, unfortunately some changes happened at her new company, her boss changed roles and Rachel's confidence started to wane.

After our third session, I could feel resistance from Rachel. The skepticism was back and I ended our call thinking she was going to send me a note saying this wasn't working for her. But she didn't and we entered our fourth session. During that session, I took a gamble and did a transformational exercise. If done too soon, sometimes people can shut down and the exercise can blow up in my face, but I followed my gut and decided to go deep, especially since I was already worried she was on her way out of my program.

During that fourth session, I asked Rachel some questions around her career path to date. The raises and promotions that didn't happen. The projects she didn't get to be a part of. How everyone else around her kept moving up. There was a lot of bitterness and resentment and I knew we had to get to the root of where this was stemming from (one of my favourite parts of coaching).

Through the transformational exercise, we uncovered that the first time Rachel felt she wasn't as good as everyone else was when she was nine and was diagnosed with diabetes. This diagnosis dramatically impacted her life and she started forming negative thoughts about her herself. Only nine at the time, Rachel formed the belief that from that moment on she would be mediocre. We talked about how she saw having diabetes as a disadvantage and that she'd never be "as good" as other people. And then: Lightbulb moment. Rachel timidly asked, "Am I holding myself back?" She realized she had unconsciously been holding herself back and inviting in rejection as it helped validate the negative thoughts she had had about herself since she was nine. Then Rachel realized she had been afraid of success her whole career. If she was successful and did well at work and got promoted, that would mean she wasn't so mediocre after all.

Rachel could accept the lie that she was mediocre and continue with the habit of holding herself back, or she could take the wheel and go after what she wanted. "I get it," she shared. "I'm the one in control of my success. No one else." BAM. That's all it took to set her on a path of greatness. In just a few months' time she was one of a few people in her company to get a raise, she got asked to lead a major project and was asked to be a mentor in her company's formal mentorship program. And she continues to chase big goals.

It's easy to place blame on people and circumstances and yes, a lot of time shitty things happen to great people, but we can dwell on them or we can learn from them and move on. There's always a choice.

Part of taking responsibility is also knowing when to move on. To move on from the boss after they repeatedly promise a raise or promotion, but never deliver. From a toxic workplace after they've yelled at you (the first time). From a company that works you to the bone, without any appreciation. From the friend who has used you one too many times. From the relationship that leaves you feeling sad and lonely more days than not.

Moving on is hard. It takes effort and guts. It can feel like your heart is breaking or that you're a failure. But you know what is worse? Staying stuck. Living a life you don't want. Knowing you have a heck of a lot of potential that isn't being used.

If you died tomorrow, what would you be remembered for? And is that what you want?

You are in the driver's seat to write your eulogy and it's not too late.

But the first step in doing so is to be aware of the behaviours or habits that need changing and to take responsibility that you are the only one who has the control to change them. You are the driver of your car. So, pull out that list of bad habits you want to change and circle one or two you're ready to tackle. Then, commit to one small action step you can take towards changing the habit.

Be you

Now that you know no one else is responsible for your success but you, let's look at who you are at your authentic core and how often that true version of you comes out.

Let's imagine for a moment that we stripped every role or every title away from you.

Daughter.

Parent.

Spouse.

Family member.

Friend.

Manager.

Boss.

Employee.

Now tell me, what's left?

Who are you?

If this question is hard to answer, don't worry, most of us don't know who we are outside of our roles, which is why I'm writing this chapter. To help you uncover it for yourself.

But first, let me share a little story.

It was 2008 and an incredibly big year for me.

That was the year I became a wife. A title I wanted and was thrilled to have. I was marrying the love of my life in my dream ceremony with a reception in my quaint hometown. My husband, Chris, and I had been living together leading up to the wedding, so really the biggest change was we now had official titles–Mr. & Mrs.–husband and wife. That's when the shift started. By assuming a new title.

I told myself this new title came with additional responsibilities. I *should* cook more, I *should* know how to sew, I *should* know how to garden, and I *shouldn't* travel so much for work. And who was telling me all this? Who was making me feel like I should or shouldn't be doing these things? Me, myself and I! Chris never asked for any of this. My parents didn't tell me to act a certain way, although my parents did have traditional, stereotypical roles. I just felt like society expected me to behave differently now that I was a wife.

I didn't enjoy cooking, I didn't know how to sew, and the last thing I wanted to do was garden. And who did enjoy all of these? Chris. I didn't want Chris to do all the work at home, but I also felt I *should* act a certain way as a wife and if I didn't, I would fail. (Hello, fear of failure.)

It was also the year I started my MBA. My work graciously gave me a leave of absence so I could focus on my eight-month accelerated program, but I had been making money consistently since I was 12 years old. Sure, not making money was temporary, and the investment would more than pay off, but now not only was I going to be a wife, but I was also going to rely on my husband's income for our first eight months of marriage. Gulp.

This was the year I started losing a bit of myself. The year I started acting how I thought I should and sadly by my own doing.

And it only got worse as I progressed in my career.

In addition to being my new title of "wife," I worked hard and got the titles of Senior Manager, managing a team, and then Director, a dream role for someone in her 30s, with a big mandate of managing teams and complex projects. It was a role I worked my butt off to get, interviewed for while jetlagged and on parental leave, and that I beat out 80 other candidates for.

But getting the dream role and beating everyone at it can do strange things to us. Downright cruel things. Things like telling yourself fake news.

It goes a little like this…

"Eighty people wanted and didn't get this job. They picked me. How exciting! But wait, oh man, they picked me. I must prove to everyone I was the right choice. I must work super long hours, say yes to everything, and show them just how good I am."

Has this ever happened to you? You get something you earned outright and then feel you have to prove yourself to others to show them that you earned it?

Or you worry they're going to figure you out—that you actually weren't deserving of the role and they might just take it away at any moment. So, you work extra hard to prove you were the right choice. This is in essence the definition of imposter syndrome.

Either way, it's exhausting. Am I right?

Oh, but wait, let me add some more roles to your title and just really confuse the hell out of you.

You're now a Mom on top of a Wife and Director.

Now, it wasn't just the pressure of acting a role at work. I also had two kids at home and a husband who did most of the caretaking.

Logically, it made sense he did more of the caretaking. We had one car, which he drove, and our daycare was a 10-minute drive away. Of course, he would do the drop-offs and pick-ups on his way to and from work. He also worked a shorter workday than me so he was able to make the dinners during the week.

Did he complain? Never!

Was I okay with it? Nope! I felt guilty as hell.

Somehow I'd reverted back to the 1950s in my mind and felt like I was letting society down by not being a more traditional mom and wife. Seriously, what the hell? As I'm writing this years later, I can see how crazy it sounds but when I was in it, it didn't seem crazy at all. I loved my work, I knew I was a better mom and wife because of it, yet I still felt bad for not being around more during the week.

Oddly enough the one time I could escape it was when I travelled for work. I knew I couldn't make it home for dinner and bedtime so on those days I was able to relax. Strange, I know.

Let's look at the flip side—what happens when your role changes or is taken away? Then what? How do you identify yourself?

While in the Director role, I thoroughly enjoyed my job but the stress and last-minute travel were taking its toll on me. I was leading a highly complex project being implemented in Latin America, which meant presenting to senior leadership every other week and flying to countries like Costa Rica, Panama, Peru and Mexico. I know it sounds glamorous, but trust me, the days were spent primarily in windowless board rooms from dusk until dawn. I did enjoy the people and team-work, though—that was fantastic!

I was headed for burnout so I did what I call pressing the easy button and reached out to a couple of friends to see what was out there, AND I accepted the first offer I got.

My new role would still be in banking but as a Senior Manager. A step down in title, a step up in pay. At the time I told myself that I wanted the less stressful job and if I was going to get paid more for it, even though it meant a "lesser" title, I was OK with that.

The thing is, title mattered to me. I was my role after all and I started to wonder how people perceived me. And, salaries aren't published, titles are.

Again, the people I worked with were great but the work didn't drive me as much as it could have. Oh, and I had declared this would be the last company I worked for. I was determined to stop company hopping and really make a name for myself here. And my manager was planning on leaving in the next little while, which meant I could take on his role. Or so I thought.

But, something strange happened to me in this role. Perhaps it wasn't the right fit culturally or perhaps it was seeing myself as "demoted" but I started to act differently than I had in my Director role. Even a colleague I'd worked with previously and who helped me get this new job pointed out that I used to speak up a lot more at the last company and how quiet I was now.

I agreed with him but couldn't pinpoint what it was that made me quieter. The only thing I could think of was early on at a planning meeting off-site, I spoke up, shared an idea I had and was greeted by deer in headlights. Did that make me shut up more? Perhaps. No one made me feel stupid but they also didn't value my idea.

A few months later my boss moved on and I spent three gruelling months interviewing for his role with my colleagues who also became quite competitive, unfortunately. I was also playing the role of Director until the spot was filled. Remember my story earlier when I mentioned I had a performance review at the same time my eldest was sick? Well, here's how the rest of that story panned out.

The day I had my performance review with my boss, I was running on little to no sleep, as I'd been up through the night with my son, who was ill (back when we still thought it was the stomach flu). My boss had two daughters and was a family guy, yet I didn't like bringing my personal stuff to work so I held back on telling him how sick my son was and how tired I felt. We entered the meeting room, sat down and he went on to tell me how well I was doing and that I'd be getting a really nice bonus. And how did I react? I started *crying*. My first time EVER crying in front of a boss. I couldn't get it under control.

Looking back on it now, I can understand how confusing the situation may have been for my boss. He gave me a good performance review and bonus and I cried, but not happy tears. He then awkwardly mentioned "services" the bank has (meaning therapy) and I cringed. That's not why I was crying. I was crying because I knew in that moment that I didn't get the promotion. It had been three months of interviews and if I was going to get it, that would have been the moment he told me. I was also telling myself that I got such a good performance review and bonus as a retention tactic. So I questioned how deserving this bonus was. I wasn't getting the promotion but they didn't want to lose me. Who knows if that was true or not but it's what happens in the corporate world, a lot.

I ended up going to the "health room" on that floor and texting a friend/colleague to come meet me. She did and was amazing, but I couldn't shake it. It was the most upset I had ever been at work. So, I went home, not knowing that would be the night Jackson would go to the hospital and that I wouldn't be back for about a month until my son was better. It was exactly the break and space I needed, although it still hurts a little to remember that time.

When I got back into the office that January (I'd been working remotely off and on), I officially found out that I didn't get the job and guess what? I felt relief. Yes, you read that correctly. I felt relief. I also felt shame and embarrassment that my colleagues would wonder what was wrong with me–how could someone who was "Acting Director" not get the role after three months? It was a blow to my self-confidence.

I didn't know who I was without a senior title anymore and I needed to find out. So, when a message came from my husband's former boss about a career retreat where you could figure out what you want to do for your "next chapter" that she was hosting with an executive coach, I jumped right on it. Sometimes we need a sign and that was mine.

I'd never worked with a coach before and I was nervous about spending the money, but it was time to get some unbiased help. It was a three-day retreat in the middle of winter on a horse farm, and the scenery was stunning. Sam, the host, made us incredible meals, and our sessions were guided by Coach Margaret beside a fireplace. The word idyllic doesn't do it justice.

I could write an entire book on my experience at the retreat so, for the sake of time, I'll leave you with my key takeaways from that weekend:

- My self-confidence had taken a much bigger hit than I realized. I had gone from beating 80 applicants for a Director role to feeling pretty darn low about my qualifications and questioning if I could ever get a senior position again.

- After getting married, I took the "easy" way out of things professionally—rather than look at how I could reduce my stress, anxiety or boredom, I changed jobs and always took the first ones that came along. I guess you might say at least I didn't stay in a role I was unhappy in, but I could have taken more time to figure out that right next move.

- I had clarity for the first time in a long time as to what I truly wanted in my career. And it was scary! I listened to my heart and finally said out loud that I wanted to be an entrepreneur. I wanted to one day have a business where I helped people live happier, healthier and more fulfilling lives. I didn't know the how yet but I did walk away with a couple of initial first steps. One included bringing my husband along for the journey. Something else I wasn't very good at. (Sorry, Chris!)

I was also given a piece of homework. I was to reach out to my friends and family and ask what they like about me. You know, as a way to boost my self-confidence.

So I did and guess what happened?

I got amazing answers back BUT they made me feel worse.

Why?

Because they were centred around my role as a working professional. Ninety percent of the replies had to do with how ambitious I was, how great I was at my job, etc. The perfect things to help someone who felt pretty down about her work, right? But I took it as "people only see me as the working professional." No one mentioned that I'm a good mom or wife or friend. My father-in-law (may he rest in peace) mentioned I'm always smiling but other than that, no one mentioned the other qualities I have that make up the me outside of work. It stung. But it was also another wake-up call that I needed.

I realized I wanted to be known for more than just my work. I wanted to be a better mom, wife and friend. I wanted to be more like Grade 5 Shannon who didn't care so much about what other people thought, who could just be, not pretend. And I started to expand on my vision. I wanted to walk my kids to and from school. I wanted to chat with other parents in the schoolyard at drop-off and pick-up. I wanted to be able to take my kids to extracurricular activities. I envisioned a job with flexibility in my schedule and hours. I envisioned what a day in the life of being my own boss could look like. A hybrid world between work and family. I envisioned standing on stages and working with individuals and groups, helping them to live happier and more fulfilling lives.

You know the ironic thing about it? Since becoming an entrepreneur I speak openly about how I pretended to be someone else for so long, and you know what I hear back? "You could have fooled me." "I had no idea you were acting." "You seemed so happy." "You came across as so confident." No wonder it was exhausting–I was an actor in my everyday life.

Now it's your turn. Where have you been letting other people drive your car or influence its direction? Where have you been holding back a piece of yourself? And are you ready to uncover the real you?

Exercise: Uncovering the Real You

Earlier we had you create that beautiful vision for your dream life with no holds barred (i.e., no restricting yourself). Now I invite you to go back to **a time in your life when you felt the happiest or most free**. For some people this was when they were a child and hadn't yet learned to dampen their desires or before they learned to be afraid of things. For others, this may be when they lived on their own for the first time, perhaps in college, or when they got their first real job and finally felt independent. Whatever it is, make sure it's a time in your life you look upon fondly. Now, close your eyes and picture stepping into that younger you. Step into their body and look out through their eyes. Looking around, what do you notice? What is this younger version doing? Feeling? Sensing? What activities do they enjoy? When they speak, how does it sound? Confident? Joyful? Carefree? What else feels important about this time? Why is it such a happy time? What makes it happy?

Next, with this vision loaded up in your mind, go ahead and answer the following questions on a piece of paper or on your phone. Take your time but don't second guess–trust that whatever comes up is the right answer.

1. What qualities do you admire about the version of you that was at her happiest?

2. What feelings were most present? What brought on those feelings?

3. What activities brought you the most joy?

4. What do you think happened to that version of you?

5. Do you want to get back that earlier version of you and if so, why? What about that feels important?

6. What might you need to let go of to do so?

If the above is hard and you don't have a time in your past that stands out as happy, I'd encourage you to look at who you admire, dead or alive, people you know or famous people and list all of the qualities you admire in them. Admiring other people can be like looking in a mirror—we admire the qualities we have inside of us, even if they're hiding.

Now answer,

1. Who are you when all your roles are stripped away?

2. What do you admire about your authentic self?

3. What qualities do you value?

4. What might you need to do to get closer to your true self?

5. And, if you didn't have to put on an act anymore and saw that people loved you for you, how might that set you free?

Drop the guilt

As we talked about in the previous chapter, you are not your role. So yes, you might have many titles—wife, mom, caretaker, boss. But that doesn't mean YOU can't be your top priority. After all, when you feel energized and passionate about your life, who wins? EVERYONE around you. Except the haters. There'll always be haters who are envious of what you have and guess what? That's OK. Because you are going to be living your dream life and you don't need anyone who's going to get in the way of that.

I'm also guessing you carry a bit of guilt when it comes to prioritizing yourself and your desires. You likely already have lots of reasons going through your head as to why you can't. So, until you can give it to yourself, I grant you full permission to go after your dream life. And sometimes, we need to hear it from someone else first before we believe we can chase our dreams. That's what happened to me a few years ago in the corporate world. Twice in fact.

Remember when I told you that I beat out over 80 applicants to get my Director role? That it was my dream title and one I'd worked towards for years? That I spent part of my parental leave preparing and interviewing for that role? The role I went back to work three months early for? Well, I loved that role. I really did. I look back at it with fondness. It challenged me in ways I never thought possible. It was also the most stressful job I ever had. I was constantly preparing decks and presenting to senior executives. I was the one who had to deliver the news when our project was delayed and take the heat. I was the one who had to hop on a plane with one to two days' notice to get stakeholder buy-in or attend a local steering committee meeting in Central or South America. And I was the one who had to lead a huge technology project from inception to execution without ever having done anything like this before. And I loved it. But this love came at a cost.

At home I had a two-year-old and a six-month-old and while I didn't resent going back to work early (I was never stay-at-home mom material), I felt immense guilt for not being the mom and wife I thought I "should" be. Looking back on it now, it was the guilt that was the hardest part. I actually enjoyed the work, travel, presenting to senior execs and the pressure that came with it. I didn't fear I would be fired but I did fear failure. I also didn't know how to manage my stress and last-minute unexpected asks that would throw my personal time with my family out of whack. That's what I couldn't handle.

Gosh how I wish someone had taught me how to create boundaries, how to stop people pleasing and how to look after my well-being earlier on in my life so I could have handled the stress and anxiety caused by my role. We spend so much time mitigating risk in the corporate world (especially in banking) as it relates to revenue, yet we don't do it for ourselves and our teams as it relates to our mindsets and mental health.

Amid this big project, I went for lunch with one of my first bosses turned mentor who still worked with the company but in a different department, and I shared everything I was going through. And by shared, I mean unloaded how miserable I was. Yes, I loved my job, but the stress and fear of failure were eating me up. I was no longer enjoying myself and I was bringing all my stress, anxiety and misery home at the end of the day. My project had another two-plus years before it would finish. That seemed like a lifetime. I'd also just had my star employee quit and I feared another one was on the way out. The pressure was mounting.

After dumping my misery on my mentor and telling her how I had two more years of this, she asked me "Why?" Why did I feel I had to stay for the two years? I was shocked. I was sure she was going to tell me to suck it up and that two years would fly by. But she didn't. She stopped me in my tracks and questioned why I didn't look at my other option: changing jobs. "I couldn't do that to the project or my boss or the team," I replied. "I would burn bridges and get a horrible reputation." Again, she questioned where my priorities lay: with my well-being and my family, or my work? I was putting my work above all else. She encouraged me to explore if there was a way to leave without burning bridges. She also asked me if there was ever really a good time to leave a job.

This mentor gave me the permission I needed to start exploring what I wanted and how I could do it in a tactful way. A few months later, I gave my boss notice but had taken the time to come up with a transition plan and a thoughtful exit strategy. And we're still friends to this day. That next role was my Senior Manager role in another bank where I told myself "This is it. This is the company I am going to spend the rest of my career at. I'm going to progress to senior roles (SVP was the most senior I ever really envisioned), I'm going to get a great pension and I will be done with interviewing and switching companies."

But the stories we tell ourselves don't always match up with what we believe deep down. Even before I left my "dream job" above, I was dreaming of being an entrepreneur. I pictured creating my own schedule and not having to answer to anyone. More importantly, I pictured not having to work on vacation or weekends when I already had plans unless I chose to do so. I pictured control and freedom. And as great as the perks are that come with working for a bank, freedom and control are not two of them, at least not at the mid-senior level where I was.

So, when my son was admitted to the hospital and I started questioning my future but was feeling guilty for doing so, I landed in a spot similar to the above. I had a belief that in the corporate world, you must be in a position for two to three years before you could ever imagine leaving it. And that belief came backed by processes that said if you applied for another job within two years of being in a role, you needed your manager's approval. (P.S., I don't love this rule.)

I felt I needed permission to pursue a new career path, and I got it from Michelle Obama. Reading her book inspired me to change my life and gave me the permission I needed to set out on a new path, albeit a different, more adventurous one this time. Michelle reminded me that just because you studied a certain subject in school and were excelling in that field, didn't mean you couldn't change paths and try something new–something that lit you up more. Thank you, Michelle.

Exercise: Granting Yourself Permission

I'd love for you to drop the guilt now and grant yourself permission to go after what you want. (I'm sure you saw that coming.) Push any negative thoughts or self-doubt aside and **write down your permission statement**. Something like:

I am a badass woman who deserves all the happiness in the world and I'm going after it.

I am big, bold and brave and go after what I want. (This is mine by the way, but feel free to use it.)

I am a confident, successful person who is fulfilling my dream of becoming X and kicking ass at it.

Your turn.

Once you have your statement, I want you to picture sharing it with someone and if that feels a little bit uncomfortable, that's a good sign. It likely means you're being bold with your affirmation. If not, is there a word or two you can add to make it stand out a bit more? Remember, we're breaking free from how we think we *should* be—we want to elicit the wow factor, not a "Awwww, that's so cute!" factor we would get from seeing a kitten. Be bold!

Dropping the guilt and giving yourself permission to chase your happy helps cement the belief that you are worth your dream life. And once you believe that the following steps and exercises become easier.

Write new stories

Did you know that each and every one of you is a creative writer? No, seriously. You are. You are fantastic when it comes to writing stories about situations in your life. Stories such as why so-and-so didn't call you back, what a line in an email means when it's not clear or why you weren't asked to sit in on a certain meeting. Every day we make up stories that are really our interpretations of what's going on in our lives. And sometimes they're true but more often than not they're fiction and tend to play off of our insecurities. And while we're on the subject, here's an example of some of my creative writing.

Last year, I had a well-paid in-person speaking gig and afterwards, I told people how incredible it went.

Except, that wasn't completely true.

The true part was I felt confident and comfortable and could ditch my notes. The attendees weren't on their phones or checked out as can happen with these events, which I took as a great sign. In other words, the audience was engaged and we had fun.

But, what else happened was that I was not the main attraction but rather a bonus at the end of the event. I've come to learn from other speakers that sometimes speakers are brought in as the main event and sometimes they're brought in to check a box that meets certain

HR criterion like "improved employee well-being" or "mental health awareness." In this case, I checked the box–the attendees were coming to hear about an update to a major project that impacted them and weren't necessarily there for me. The event ended up running extremely behind schedule and as the last person up, I made the executive decision to cut my talk short to respect the attendees' time. Once I was done, only one person came up to me to tell me how much they appreciated my talk. As I always do, I emailed the organizers of the event when I got home to thank them and ask for feedback but didn't hear back.

So, what happened next?

I ruminated–I told myself maybe I wasn't so great after all and the event coordinators weren't sure how to tell me so they opted not to respond. I questioned my material. I questioned if I got too vulnerable with my stories–perhaps it was too much. I finally wrote down how I was feeling and reminded myself that I had to be okay with not getting feedback and move on.

And guess what? A couple of weeks later I got an email from the coordinators with great feedback saying the attendees enjoyed the event. They even included some of the key takeaways the participants had. And you know why they waited? They were waiting for the event survey results to come in. Doh! I had taken their silence to mean I didn't do a good job. But in this case, the coordinators were just busy and wanted to wait for the survey results to come in so they could provide more concrete feedback. After all, I had asked for that in my thank you email to them.

How often do we take silence as rejection? Or a sign of failure? What stories do we tell ourselves in those moments? That we suck or they didn't like us? And then how silly do we feel when we do finally hear back and the news we get is the opposite of what we told ourselves?

Well, dear readers, it's time to tell yourself new stories.

You have the vision of what lights you up, you are taking responsibility, you have a better sense of who you are at your core, you're giving yourself permission and you have the tools to overcome a lot of the obstacles on your path. Now it's time to do another soul-searching exercise so you can take off your armour and shine like a kid with all the confidence in the world.

How can we do that? By focusing on you and all of your awesomeness. You are the only you who will ever be born and what a blessing you are to this world and the people around you. Unfortunately, along your life's journey, you experienced negative experiences and comments that might have chipped away at your confidence and little pieces of you. But you can get it all back and more!

Every single one of us has some emotional scarring from our childhood, either from our parents, siblings, friends or school bullies. Heck, if that wasn't the case, we wouldn't need therapists and coaches in this world. The reality is you never know what comment or situation is going to create a long-lasting negative belief. I'm sure I've already left some imprints on my kids, for better or worse.

The same applies as adults. You can have one horrible boss say one stupid comment to you and bam, you've turned that idiot's comment into a truth which turned into a belief you now hold true.

I remember once being told I wasn't very strategic and until I was more strategic, I wouldn't move ahead.

The comment "you're not strategic" wasn't true. What was true was that I was leading a dysfunctional team where I was doing way more hands-on work than I should have as we were short of people and I didn't have time to be strategic. I would have loved to spend parts of my day coming up with strategies on how to move the business forward, but at the time I didn't have the bandwidth nor the energy to do so.

So the comment of me not being strategic wasn't true. I wasn't "acting" strategic at the time, but it didn't mean I didn't have it in me. Words carry a lot of weight and being and doing are two different things.

Okay, time to get uncomfortable.

What words or phrases have you said to yourself today? This week? This year? When you look at yourself in the mirror, what are your initial thoughts? Perhaps comments about your weight, your hair colour, your hair cut, your skin? If you need to, pull out the lists you made in *What Holds Us Back*.

You could lose weight.

Your skin is really thinning out.

Your roots look awful.

What do you say to yourself after a meeting goes south or you didn't land a job, client or project you worked really hard for?

You don't know what you're doing.

You should never have opened your mouth.

You're going to get fired.

How about in your relationships when someone doesn't text back right away?

They hate me.

I must have said something that pissed them off.

I bet they're all hanging out talking about me right now.

Oh my gosh, how often have I told myself stories about people who didn't respond for a little while only to hear "I'm so sorry for the delay in responding. I was out with the stomach flu. I wanted to tell you how much fun I had with you the other night."

Then what happens? We immediately tell ourselves more negative things like *Shannon, you're so ridiculous, as if you thought she didn't like you. You are so dramatic.*

And the vicious cycle goes round and round and round.

Some people know what obstacles are in their way, and which beliefs hold them back. But many people have blind spots. Their beliefs are so deep inside, they need help to uncover them. (Remember my fear of loss and how it took a therapist to uncover it?) Or, people are afraid to name their beliefs for fear of then having to confront them. They fear opening a can of worms.

I get it. These are valid concerns. The thing is, these beliefs or stories are probably doing more damage inside than you know. And does pretending they're not there make them disappear? Hell no! So, it is time to open that can and let the worms out. Then we can eliminate them until they no longer stand in our way (metaphorically speaking of course).

Exercise: Facing Your Stories

In order to break the cycle, we have to do something pretty drastic and sad.

1. **I'd like you to list all of the negative things you say to yourself.** Personally, professionally, physically, mentally. Put them all down on a piece of paper or in the notes section of your phone.

Things like:

I'm ugly.
I need to lose weight.

My outfit looks ridiculous.
I sounded stupid in class yesterday.
My friends all talk about me behind my back.
I suck at presenting.
I should be further ahead at work.
I'm a failure.
I'm not good enough.

2. **Then picture someone you love and read this list of negative things out loud as if you are saying it to them.** (If you have a kid, I'd encourage you to picture them for this exercise. Note, you're not actually saying these things to them, but you're pretending).

    You're ugly.
    You need to lose weight.
    Your outfit looks ridiculous.
    You sounded stupid in class yesterday.
    Your friends all talk about you behind your back.
    You suck at presenting.
    You should be further ahead at work.
    You're a failure.
    You're not good enough.

3. **Notice how it feels** to say these things out loud to someone you love or to say them to a 10-year-old kid. Stay with the sadness, hurt and ickyness that comes up. Let it sink in how horrible we are to ourselves on an on-going basis. Feel it and acknowledge it.

If you were a parent who said these things to your kid, it would be verbal abuse. Now I know that sounds harsh but it's true.

So why oh why do we talk to ourselves this way? No wonder 85% of people suffer from self-esteem issues,[17] according to self-esteem expert and author Dr. Joe Rubino. Geez. We all need therapy to overcome self-induced trauma!

Exercise: Writing New Stories

Now, let's take your creative writing skills and write some new stories to get you closer to your vision. Here are four steps to take:

1. **Start catching yourself.** Every time you hear that mean voice in your head, you're going to tell that voice to shut it. (Perhaps even give it a name, like Bertha–sorry to any Berthas reading this but that's the first name that popped up for me where I don't know any.)

2. **Then, ask yourself–is this story fact or fiction?** Would it hold up in a court of law or is it something you've come to believe as true but lack proof?

3. **Now pay yourself a compliment, but a genuine one you can believe.** The only way we are going to be kinder to ourselves is to increase our self-empathy. (And let's add this word to our regular vocab while we're at it–*self-empathy*; I like it.)

4. **Write new stories.** It's time for the secret ingredient, y'all. I hope you're ready because this is the real game changer in

life. *This is the most important part of this book I want you to walk away with.* Because without this secret ingredient, we will never truly unleash our inner beauty onto this world!

That secret ingredient (drum roll, please) is to reframe those beliefs you're telling yourself and tell yourself new, positive stories instead. Take all those negative stories you tell yourself that you listed above and throw them in the garbage. You're getting rid of them so you can write new stories, better stories. Stories that are going to get you to where you want to go.

Let's look at some examples of how to flip your negative beliefs to positive ones.

I don't have time → I have time for what I prioritize.

I suck at presenting → I am getting better at presenting every day.

My face is getting wrinkly → I look freaking fantastic for my age.

I'm not as thin as I used to be → I have one hell of a strong body that gave me two beautiful babies.

I'm too quiet → I speak up for what matters.

I don't have the right experience → I have a kick-ass resumé that is going to land the right job for me.

I should be further ahead at work → I am gaining the experience I need for where I'm headed.

I'm not good enough → I am one incredible human exactly as I am.

I could go on and on, but I'll stop there.

Now it's your turn, your turn to take that list of negative things you tell yourself on a regular basis and write down a new story for every single item. It will likely feel uncomfortable and that's OK. It's supposed to. If it were comfortable, we would be telling ourselves compliments on a more regular basis.

Remember to look at the examples above when you're writing your new stories. Notice how all of the reframes are stated in the positive. I didn't just add a "not" as the reframe. That's because our subconscious doesn't do a great job of differentiating positive or negative thoughts and may still focus on the negative words. You want to ensure you're creating a lovely list of new beliefs that should bring a warm feeling as you read them, even if they feel a tad uncomfortable.

5. **Lastly, take your new, positive stories and copy them onto a fresh piece of paper or put them in the notes section of your phone.** Now for the uncomfortable part—you're going to read these positive reframes out loud to yourself every day. Why? Because it takes time for your heart to catch up to your thoughts. It takes time to believe what you're stating as true, but repetition works (hello, brainwashing). And when you catch a negative story creeping in, remember to add it to your list and write a new story for it.

Now that you've done one of the hardest exercises in this book, I invite you to do a little dance or do as motivational speaker and coach Mel Robbins would say, go give yourself a high five in the mirror. You are doing the hard work required to get you closer to your dreams. So be proud and celebrate your wins along the way. That will help you continue to do the hard work, like what's coming up next.

Confront the elephant in the room

With all of the wonderful stories you're now starting to tell yourself, it's time to confront the elephant in the room—the other F word: FEAR.

Tim Ferriss, an American entrepreneur and author, brought this concept to life for me in his TED Talk "Why you should define your fears instead of your goals." Tim talked about how we will never achieve our goals if we don't first identify our fears and work to overcome them. By defining the fears getting in the way of our success, we can do the work to break through or overcome them. But without doing that crucial step, we will continue to hold ourselves back.

Leveraging Tim's concept, I now do an exercise with all my clients to define not only their fears but also any other obstacles they have—worries, excuses, beliefs, bad habits. We get them all out on a spreadsheet during a session and then go through them one by one. And wow, is there something about saying our obstacles out loud and seeing them on paper that is pretty darn powerful.

Often, just by asking my clients what's the worst thing that could happen if they face their obstacle, they quickly realize that by talking about the elephant in the room and getting it on paper, it's usually not as bad as they thought. Sometimes it's the push they need to get out of their own way. Like what happened with Serena.

I start every call with my clients by asking them to share a win they've had for the week. My clients sometimes tell me that's the hardest question I ask but when it came to Serena, in just her first session, she had one at the ready. Serena excitedly told me how she finally spoke up in a client meeting and asked her client some tough questions. Normally she would hold back when her boss was there for fear of looking stupid or making her boss look bad, but this time she didn't. And guess what happened? She sparked an incredible conversation with her client and the other people at the table.

I loved how proud Serena was of herself when she shared her story with me. When I asked what made the difference for her to be able to speak up this time, she shared how when she and I first met in her discovery session, I'd asked her to think of the worst-case scenario when she felt fear and if she was okay with that worst-case, then to go for it. As Serena later shared with me, in just five minutes during her free discovery session, I guided her to see another perspective she hadn't previously seen. I had her fess up and name the elephant in the room when it came to speaking up (aka her fear). And what happens when we name the elephant? We take its power away.

Serena had told herself her biggest fear of speaking up was looking like an idiot, but once she said it out loud she quickly realized that the fear was fake—it was an insecurity that wasn't real. She already had a seat at the table at her work so of course she wasn't an idiot. She decided in that moment, the fear of being an idiot would no longer hold her back. She spoke up and she crushed it! Sometimes all it takes is acknowledging our fears and going through the different scenarios to see they're not as scary as we make them out to be, which in turn gives us the guts to take them for a test drive.

In my case, I have two things that get my palms sweaty, my stomach doing somersaults and my heart racing, but once they're over, I'm on an incredible high. Those two things are physical activities and public speaking. Yup, two pretty opposite things, I know.

With physical activities, my anxieties boil down to two things—I don't want to get injured, and I don't want to let my team down if it's a team sport. For public speaking, I don't want to look stupid or waste people's time if what I'm saying bores them or doesn't deliver on the ask.

But that natural high that comes after I've done them is oh so worth it. And if I don't have things in my life that excite or scare me from time to time, I tend to experience boredom, which leads to excessive TV watching, drinking and eating.

So, at the start of 2021, I set a goal to do more things that excite or scare me. I made these goals partly because I found myself holding myself back at times, caring too much about what others thought (hello, 3 P's), and because I've learned that those natural highs are what fulfill me and thus lead to healthier habits.

Interesting, isn't it, how something we find scary can be the same thing that genuinely fills our cup and leaves us wanting more?

It's just a matter of overcoming those obstacles that come between us and that fulfillment.

So, on New Year's Day, I wrote down what I wanted to leave behind in 2020 on individual pieces of paper so I could do more of what excites and scares me—letting go of self-doubt and caring so much about what others think. I then took those pieces of paper and threw them into a bonfire. It felt fantastic! And vulnerable. Vulnerable because I did it on video and then shared these things with my family and on social media.

I wanted to hold myself accountable and one way to do that is by sharing our goals with others. Plus, I wanted to set an example for my boys that we should try things even if they're scary. They'll tell you one of my favourite sayings is to try one thing every day that scares you (especially when standing in line at Canada's Wonderland, a large amusement park in Canada). In 2021, I tried a lot of things that scared me.

Here are a few examples of things I tried in 2021 that were outside my comfort zone in case they spark any ideas for you:

- Presenting for a big client pitch.

- Sharing my struggles with anxiety on LinkedIn.

- Quitting my corporate job and an excellent and stable income to pursue my dream of being an entrepreneur and having the flexibility to spend more time with my kids.

- Trail biking for the first time.

- Going on The Bat at Canada's Wonderland–a large rollercoaster that goes backwards and upside down (and screaming so loud my youngest son heard me a few rides away).

- Posting vulnerable videos on social media.

- Trying a new water slide at a water park.

- Attending a three-day retreat in Northern Ontario to reconnect with my inner child without knowing a single person.

- Water skiing for the first time since I was a kid and finally getting up after six attempts, even if it was just for a second.

- Pitching my business and articles to individuals and companies.

Have I loved every second of it? Nope. But have I learned from my experience? You bet.

Here are some of my learnings to date:

- I have had a ton of fun. Whether it was with my family on adventures or from meeting new people and trying new things, it has been a blast!

- The process isn't always fun–it can mean letting people down or seeing people's true colours, but the end goal is usually worth it.

- Rejection is hard but short-lived–take what you can learn from it and move on.

- The more you do it, the more comfortable it becomes, although it doesn't mean you'll grow to love it, and that's OK.

- The pain is worth the gain. The sweaty palms, thinking you're going to be sick, feeling short of breath—all of these suck, but the natural high that comes after or with a win is worth every second of it.

Well, friend, it's time to open that can of worms and confront the elephant in your room, even if it feels uncomfortable, embarrassing or sad. As we talked about earlier and as poet Robert Frost said, "The best way out is through."

Exercise: Facing Your Fears

1. I want you to list all the things that scare the crap out of you. Personally and professionally. I want you to write them all down. Every single thing. They can be physical things like public speaking, bears, driving on the highway, losing your job or friends, or they can be more emotional like looking stupid, getting rejected, feeling less than, etc. Be sure to go back to your lists from *What Holds Us Back* to make sure you're not forgetting any.

2. Beside each elephant, list the impact it has had on you—how has this elephant held you back or gotten in your way?

3. Beside the impact, write down the worst thing that could happen if this fear/worry/belief comes true. For example, could you die? Could you get embarrassed? Could you lose your job or friends? Could you lose your house?

4. On the flip side, what's the best case scenario that could happen if you no longer let these obstacles impact you? If you can overcome this fear, what are all the glorious results you could achieve? Write those down beside each worst case.

5. Looking at your list of fears, which ones are you ready to tackle? Which best case scenarios light you up enough to break free of the obstacle? Perhaps choose your top three to tackle first and then go back for more. Next, put a star beside those three and then list one small action step for each of the three that you can take for a test drive.

Remember in *What Holds Us Back* I shared that I measure my fears by asking myself can I die from doing this? If the answer is yes, that's a hard no for me. But if the answer is no, then I ask myself if I can live with the worst-case scenario. More often than not, I can and you can too.

Get your priorities straight

Ok, you have your vision, you're in the driver's seat, you're ready to free your true self, you've given yourself permission to soar, you're writing new kick-ass stories about yourself, and you've sent fear packing. Now, let's take some action!

One of the reasons I wanted to write this book was to help people like you excel in your careers and lives but not at the expense of your well-being or family. And what's a top way to do that? Get your priorities straight and then stick to them.

How many of you have had a boss, friend or family member start down a path that you got super excited and onboard with, only to have them completely change direction? The number of times this happened when I worked in corporate was super frustrating. You'd work your butt off for hours on a presentation, only to have your boss change direction and BAM, you were back to square one. Oh my gosh, one presentation I once worked on had 87 versions and I'm talking about a long-ass document, not a few pages. And while I was getting paid to do the work, the revising of the versions caused us to start staying until 10 p.m. or later at the office, something I was NOT okay with, especially with two small kids at home.

People have a right to change direction but the trend I've noticed is this: Change of direction tends to happen more when people don't take the time to sit down and first figure out the priorities. The priorities in your life and career, of a project, of a meeting, of a renovation, etc.

That's why one of the exercises I do with all my clients is what I call *The Big Five*. The Big Five are the top five priorities, personally and professionally combined, that you want to focus on in your life at a particular point in time. Many of my clients fall into one of two camps when it comes to this exercise:

1. They have a hard time identifying their priorities or picking just five, or

2. They know their priorities but don't have their life aligned with them, which often leads to unhappiness, burnout and resentment.

Another common trait I've seen is people forgetting to include themselves on their list of priorities (picture the palm to face emoji). If you're not prioritizing yourself, you're never going to do the things you want to do or go after your dreams. You'll continue to put them on the back burner.

But naming our priorities isn't enough. We also need to understand what focusing on these big five priorities will do for us. Otherwise—you guessed it—we will change them the next time a bright shiny ball comes by that seems like a better option.

I am definitely guilty of this, especially when I started my own business. It was now up to me to set my priorities and if I wanted to change them, I had full control. Now, that might sound super exciting, especially for any of you in a job where your manager sets your priorities at work. However, for an entrepreneur, it can be dangerous. I would set out on one path and then have someone give me some advice or share a new trend they'd seen and oops, next thing I knew I was chasing a bright, shiny new ball. While that can be fun, it can mean chasing a lot of different paths at the expense of potentially burning out or never doing one thing really well.

On the personal side, I didn't prioritize my well-being for years. I knew that eating balanced meals, sleeping well and exercising were good for me. But I equated them with losing weight or looking good. I didn't equate them with feeling energized, having more focus, lowering my stress and anxiety or being more productive.

A lot of my bosses ate like crap, didn't exercise and worked super long hours. And they were really successful. Or at least what I used to define as successful–advancing and being recognized in your career. What we don't always see is the impact on their well-being, how much time they spend with their family and friends and how present they are when they do or how happy and fulfilled they feel inside.

Similarly, many of the icons I looked up to–Ruth Bader Ginsburg (former Associate Justice of the Supreme Court of the U.S.), Warren Buffett (CEO of Berkshire Hathaway and self-made billionaire), Phil Knight (founder of Nike)–were incredible change makers and success-ful in their fields, but at a cost to their families or well-being. Or at least that's my personal opinion based on what I've read about them. Ruth Bader Ginsburg, for example, worked extremely long hours, slept very little during the week and then spent her weekends catching up on her sleep. Phil Knight also worked around the clock and admitted to not being very present with family. Warren Buffett has McDonald's for breakfast every day and has a hard time being present with his family. Being a change maker or leader can come at a cost and if you are okay with that, go for it. But if you aren't, you'll want to ensure that you know what your priorities are and then align your life with them.

But the story that stuck with me most about getting your priorities straight was that of Stacey Mowbray. Stacey, the then-CEO of Second Cup, spoke at an event during the first week of my MBA program at the Schulich School of Business, in which she shared parts of her career journey. While I don't remember all of the details, I do remember Stacey's story of how she worked her way up from a manager to a VP role in a fast-paced, high-stress job and that she was constantly running from one priority to the next.

She hadn't realized how much of a toll her career was taking on her life, however, until she dropped her five-year-old daughter off at school one day. Stacey was in a rush to get to work and when her daughter wanted to ask her something when she got out of the car, Stacey told her she didn't have time, she was going to be late for work. Her daughter then turned around and immediately dropped her shoulders in sadness. Seeing the impact she'd had on her daughter and the person she had become as a result of her work, Stacey hired a life coach to help her figure out what was important to her, and for the first time took a step back and evaluated her life. With the coach, she explored her values and defined her priorities. Once those were set, she aligned her life accordingly. Stacey moved on from her current role to an even larger role with a culture and environment that aligned with her values.

Stacey went on to share about how later she became the President and CEO of Second Cup and how important balance was to its culture, but the picture of her daughter is what sat with me. It was in that moment that I knew I wanted to be successful in my career but not at the expense of my family. Stacey proved to me that you could rise the ranks and still be a great mom and wife.

Intrigued as I was by her story for so many years, I reached out to Stacey and asked her if I could interview her for this book. Being the incredible and humble person that she is, she agreed and what she shared with me inspired me even more.

Stacey told me that one of the biggest obstacles she faced in her career was *not feeling adequate about anything she was doing*. She didn't feel like a good mother, wife or employee. She also wasn't great at managing her stress and would bring it home with her at the end of the day causing her to be short with her family. In turn, this created a tense and stressful environment for her whole family.

What I love most about Stacey's story is that she didn't have to shy away from success to stick to her values and priorities. She just had to find a role and a company that was aligned with them. As Stacey says, "Bigger roles don't always mean more stress if the culture and role align with what's important in your life." That's what the role of CEO of Second Cup was for her. She was able to show up as her true self and had less stress as a result.

Another strategy Stacey explored with her coach was to make five-year plans so she could map out her future. One of her plans was to live abroad for work at some point in her career. And in 2014, once her daughters were older, that dream came to life when Stacey went on to serve as the President for WW (formerly WeightWatchers) and got to move from Toronto to New York City. Now, Stacey is back in Toronto living her other dream of sitting on five different Boards of Directors and imparting all of the wisdom she has gained over the course of her career. Stacey continues to set five and 10 year plans that are more holistic, looking at how she wants to live and the impact she wants to have. Her two daughters grew into wonderful, balanced women and she has an amazing relationship with both of them. Identifying her values, priorities, plans and dreams are what set Stacey on her path to success.

Your turn! If you checked in with your gut right now, what does it tell you that you want if it doesn't mean adding more stress or busyness to your life? If you could go for something that was more aligned with your values and priorities, what would that be? And who is a role model that you can look to while still being you?

Part of my challenge was I didn't have one until I heard Stacey speak that first time in 2008. Before that, I'd never heard someone in a leadership role speak so openly and vulnerably about the struggles working moms face. But from that moment on, I've held Stacey in the back of my mind throughout my career. Interestingly, when I mentioned her to one of my clients who is younger than me and in a different phase of his life, he mentioned he had heard Stacey speak while at university and her talk stuck with him too.

But Stacey's story wasn't enough to inspire me to better manage my priorities–it took finally having bosses and colleagues who prioritized their well-being for me to finally make that a priority for myself. They shared their experiences of how it helped turn their brains off and helped them manage stress and that is what I needed to hear. It wasn't about looking good for me; it was that I wanted to feel more energy and feel less stressed. I also started thinking about how I wanted to be strong and healthy for my kids, which meant taking better care of my body. I had family and friends diagnosed with cancer and it scared the crap out of me. I knew I had to do better, for myself and for my family.

Finally I could see the value and I had the motivation, but I still didn't align my schedule to my priorities because I didn't believe I had the *time* to be healthy. I could scroll social media or binge-watch TV, yet I told myself there was no time for exercise. It makes zero sense but that's what we do. We lie to ourselves so much, we believe it. Remember all the excuses we talked about at the start of the book? Yeah, those ones.

We get to prioritize what we have time for and if we're choosing watching TV over working out, we are *choosing* to prioritize TV.

So let's get clear on your priorities and then we can explore ways to align your life to them. Yes, it may mean making hard choices but they'll be worth it in the long run when you can live your life in greater alignment with what you *actually* want.

Exercise: Identifying Your Priorities

Let's start with a brainstorm. Write down all the things that come to you when I ask you to choose your priorities right now. You can even start with big buckets and then narrow them down. Perhaps you choose family, work, yourself, friends and money. *Now, what is it about each item that is important to you?*

Here are some examples, but I urge you to please choose what feels best for you. And let's put a time frame on them. Let's look at your priorities for the next month and then you can work your way up from there.

- Family—Do you want to have more family dinners where you all sit around the table and are present? Perhaps it's planning a family vacation, playing with your kids more without any devices present, visiting or calling your parents once a week.

- Work—Do you have a big presentation you want to nail, or a difficult conversation with your boss you'd like to have? Maybe you want to be a more empathetic leader or work less hours?

- Yourself—Perhaps you crave alone time, or you want to start meditating or exercising. Maybe you want to find a hobby.

- Friends—Do you see your friends too much? Too little? Perhaps you have some toxic friends in your life so you're looking for more meaningful connections? Maybe you want to plan a fun night out once a month?

- Money—this can be sticking to a budget, talking to a financial planner, increasing your debt repayment amount or perhaps selling a bunch of stuff you don't need in your house anymore. Or maybe you're ready to ask for that raise!

Now, write down your *Big Five* and commit to them. Have them available in multiple places—your phone, a sticky note on your desk, a note for your kitchen or your car. Have a copy for each place you frequent often. Why? Because in order to create boundaries to align your time, energy and money to your priorities (coming up shortly), you need to have constant reminders of what they are. And while you're at it, why not share your Big Five with the important people in your life—if it helps, perhaps ask them to help hold you accountable to them.

Before we talk about how to set boundaries to help you stick to your priorities, I want to share another story about a friend of mine.

Dr. Monique Reddington learned about prioritizing her well-being the hard way in December 2020. A family doctor with two young kids and a husband who's a psychiatrist at a hospital, Mo (short for Monique) was used to juggling many balls at once. Having gone back to work early after having each of her kids, Mo was used to being busy and getting it all done. But then COVID hit and her already heavy workload (professionally and personally) became even heavier and new challenges emerged. Mo now had to deal with being exposed to patients with COVID and treating them during her clinics and in-patients, while taking on more responsibility at home as her husband's workload increased by 30%. On top of it all, she now had to be a teacher and help her kids with their online schooling.

What happens when you're busy taking care of everybody else? You forget to take care of yourself. When Mo felt her fingers and feet tingling one day, she knew she had to get to the emergency department. She thought she was having a seizure. As the doctors ran tests, Mo did what many high-achieving people-pleasers do—she was still thinking about work and texting her colleagues about her patients. She even offered to still do her rounds while waiting for results. Luckily, her colleagues said no. What Mo didn't share with anyone at the time was that she actually thought she was dying and made a video for her kids telling them how much she loved them.

Mo wasn't dying, nor did she have a chronic illness. Mo was having a panic attack. A panic attack from trying to do it all and not looking after herself. In fact, her test results showed she had barely eaten in days. Mo didn't believe her doctor. She didn't believe it could happen to her. And what came next was even harder for Mo. She was told she had to take some time off and focus on her well-being. While Mo understood taking time off would be good for her, it made her feel like a failure. It also made her feel sad, that she couldn't help her colleagues in such a busy and uncertain time. She had never believed rest was productive and was now being ordered to rest. But she didn't have a choice and she knew that it was time to start taking care of herself so she could take care of her family.

During this downtime, Mo started exercising regularly and reading self-help books. She started eating and sleeping better and spent a lot of time with her kids. She also got better at setting boundaries and asking for help, which initially felt selfish but proved essential to her well-being.

Mo did the hard work, set her priorities and then built and stuck to her boundaries and she's a better mom, wife and doctor because of it.

Creating boundaries

Now that you have your priorities, it's time to create the boundaries that will set you up for success and ensure you align your time and energy with your priorities. Let's give you a system so you know what to say yes or no to and how to better manage your schedule and to-do's. But first, let's look at the impact on priorities and boundaries in your life up until now.

How has not setting or sticking to priorities and boundaries impacted your life? What have you said no to as a result? What have you missed out on? How many sleepless nights have you had over things like this?

On the flip side, what benefits might you see and feel when you can create and stick to boundaries? What new opportunities might come up? What can you do then that you can't do now? What might you be able to say yes to? How would that feel? Who else might benefit?

I want you to keep these in mind as we consider setting boundaries to support your priorities for your life. Different areas of your life need different boundaries. There are many experts out there with many different types of boundary classifications but for the purposes of this book, I've identified four kinds: time, people, task and personal space.

Time boundaries

Time boundaries are–you guessed it–protecting how you spend your time as best as you can. Remember, your boundaries need to align with your priorities.

If having dinner with your kids is a priority, be sure to block out your calendar to make it home on time or to not be double booked into a meeting. If doing a workout at lunch three times a week is a priority, put it in your schedule. If you want to have uninterrupted, focus time for work, don't give in and say yes when a colleague asks if you can meet during your blocked off time. Say no! And remember, no is a complete sentence. You don't owe an explanation.

The best solution here is to take a few moments at the start of every month to evaluate your calendar and then continue to do it weekly. Did you overcommit yourself? Do you need to go back and decline certain events or asks? Yes, saying no is hard but if it means you get to stick to your priorities, what might change in your life?

And if you're committing to stopping work at a certain time or being present while watching your kid's hockey game, turn the notifications off your phone and put it away. The phone will win every time if you let it. Don't.

People boundaries

People boundaries can be a bit more tricky to navigate. There are certain people in our lives that suck out all of our energy when we're with them. I'm sure you're already thinking of someone right now. Perhaps it's your mother-in-law or boss who seeks and loves drama. Maybe it's a friend of yours who you should have kicked to the curb long ago but haven't had the guts to do so. The friend who only wants to gossip about other people, which makes you wonder what she says behind your back.

An ideal scenario here would be to completely remove these people from your life. But I know for many of you that just isn't possible, especially if it's someone like, say, your sister, whom you love but who also drives you nuts.

Take a moment and think of the people who drain your energy or leave you feeling down or exhausted after they leave. I picture those cartoons where the villain sucked someone's powers out of their body and left them as a puddle. Who are these people that suck your energy and powers? Take note of them and be sure to watch how often you're seeing or speaking with them.

On weeks when you know you're going to be drained by these people, be sure to set up some dates with people who give you energy or at least get ready to call them when you're on your way home to recharge some of your battery. Just be careful you don't become that constant energy suck for someone else as a result of your energy vacuums.

And if you're feeling gutsy and ready to cut the ties with that person in your life who makes you feel worse after hanging out, now is the time. You got this!

Task boundaries

Ok, let's talk *task boundaries*.

There are always going to be tasks in our lives we just really don't like. Things like laundry, cleaning, dishes, making lunches, taking minutes for a meeting, performance reviews, presenting, sales calls, etc.

With each of these things you have three choices:

1. Suck it up and get it over with.

2. Outsource or delegate it.

3. Just stop doing it.

Oh, how I wish my house duties could go into the "just stop doing it" category but unfortunately, they cannot. Not unless I want to become a hoarder and end up on the news or a reality show. However, many things in our lives can be outsourced, delegated or stopped. But sometimes making that choice is hard. It can mean something's not fully in our control or it may mean making some drastic changes like switching jobs or companies.

How many of you reading this right now wished your partners or team did more of their share of the work? How many of you get envious of the people in your lives whose partners make the lunches, get the kids ready in the morning or do the laundry? How many of you don't ask for help or delegate out of fear that the thing won't get done right? Let me ask you this, so what? What is the worst that can happen if someone does something and it's not done exactly how you would do it? Perhaps you'll need to spend more time with that person and explain how it can be done differently. Or perhaps your daughter's outfit isn't what you would have chosen to the point you want to put a sign on her letting people know her mom did not pick her outfit. To that, I'll ask again, so what? What did you get out of not having to do that task? You got time and energy back. And once you get over whether the thing was done right, you can hopefully have some peace of mind knowing you can ask for help.

Let's take a moment and look at your work tasks. What are you doing that you could delegate to someone else? What could be a great learning opportunity for somebody and free up some of your time? Sure, it takes time to train someone to do it but that time is an investment in both your life and your employee's future. What tasks can you stop doing at work? What meetings are pointless? Do you need your status meetings as often as you have them? Do you have lots of "make work" projects? Projects that require a lot of effort to complete but are pretty pointless at the end of the day. Can you challenge their purpose? Propose a less time-consuming alternative? The next time you see a million emails going back and forth on the same topic, can you pick up the phone, take five minutes and resolve the issue? Do you let people know your expectations when you task them with something? Do you understand what's expected of you with every ask? The more upfront and clear we can be with our communication, the more time and energy we will save. Plus, who likes getting to the end of a project only to find out it's not at all aligned to what their boss or client was thinking. Ugh. So frustrating!

Looking ahead at your calendar and to-do's for the coming weeks, how many things do you enjoy versus feeling you "have to" or "should" do them? One quick tip here: As soon as you find yourself saying I "should" or "have to" do something, watch out–it's an energy suck. Similar to the other boundaries above, ensure to balance your energy as much as you can, especially on the more draining weeks.

Personal space boundaries

Last but not least, we have *personal space boundaries*. Before COVID, I'm not sure this one would have made my list but what I want to talk about here is how you interact with others. And this has been made more complex since COVID as many companies have different ways of working than before. You may be working fully remote, in a hybrid setting or have been mandated back into the office. Whatever your situation is, I want you to think about your ideal situation. Are you someone who thrives off in-person socialization and contact? Do you enjoy your commute to work and being in the hustle of traffic or public transit? Do you prefer silence for your work or a noisy background?

We used to not have much say over our work environments. But now that we do, we can ask ourselves, is our work environment conducive to what we enjoy? And if not, what can we do to change that?

If spending more time with your family is a priority, and you feel working in an office is unproductive or inefficient, maybe you can talk with your boss or manager about adjusting some of your boundaries to balance your priorities and obligations. Maybe you spend a couple of days at home each week, with focused productive time and no commute, so you can get through your responsibilities quicker and have more time with your family. Then you can feel good about spending more time connecting with your colleagues and teammates on the days when you are at the office.

Understanding your personal space preferences and seeing if your current situation aligns with them could have a greater impact on your joy than you realize and the sooner you can take the steps to create alignment, the sooner you'll feel more free.

Exercise: Setting Boundaries

What are the top things getting in your way when it comes to prioritizing your Big Five? Is it time, people, tasks, personal space or perhaps all of the above? If all, what are the ones most impacting you today? The sooner you can identify which ones aren't in alignment with meeting your priorities, the sooner you can make adjustments.

Next, what steps do you need to take to create the boundaries that will help you stay on track and turn your vision into a reality? What can you commit to right here and now that you're willing to do? And when are you going to do it by? Write it down, share it with a friend and hold yourself accountable to it.

Yes, implementing boundaries is hard–it may mean saying no, disappointing people, pushing back, speaking up–but aren't you and your priorities worth it?

Quit the 3 P's

Now that you have your priorities set and know the boundaries you need to create, it's time to quit the three P's—*perfectionism, people-pleasing and perception*—as these will always get in the way of sticking to our priorities and boundaries.

This chapter is an invitation to STOP. Stop giving 110% to everything when you don't have 110% in you to give. Stop striving for perfection. Stop people pleasing. Stop caring so much about what others think. START DOING YOU! Imagine a world where everyone could show up as their true selves—how incredible would that be? How great would it be to see people acting more confidently? How much happier would everyone be as a society if we stopped caring so goddamn much about what others think of us, while still being good, kind people.

I'm not saying we shouldn't consult with others or stop looking for input on certain things, especially in the business world where collaboration and different perspectives can dramatically improve a product or project. And checking out dress codes for events is totally okay too. But, when it comes to things like our looks, style, hobbies, career paths and whom we hang out with, let's stop looking for permission, shall we? Let's start doing more of what brings us joy and what sets us free.

Set realistic expectations

I am a big believer that by being more realistic with our expectations, we can improve our happiness and focus more on the things that matter.

How often do you finish a project or initiative and then immediately start thinking of how you could have made it better or what you would change about it? We all do it, it's in our nature. But here's the thing, we only have a finite amount of time and energy and at some point, we have to decide that–like Sheryl Sandberg says–*done is better than perfect.* That rewriting an email 20 times, changing the font and colours on our slides or trying on a fifth new outfit is not going to make or break something. That if anything, striving for perfection is taking us away from something else–time spent with loved ones, being present, starting the next project.

When you give 110% of yourself to something–your job, your client, your kids–do you get 110% in return? Do you get paid more than your salary or fee? Do your kids acknowledge all your efforts? Sometimes, sure, but more often than not, we don't get an incremental 10% return and if anything, it cost us.

Because our time and energy are limited resources, we want to be sure we're spending them on the right priorities. The things that will get us closer to our dreams, not further away.

How do we do that? By acknowledging what you can give to a certain area on a daily, weekly or monthly basis. If you have a big deliverable at work, lower the amount of yourself that you give at home. Alternatively, if something is happening in your personal life, like caring for a sick parent or child, or if your partner is going through his or her busy season, it might mean your work goes on the back burner for a little while. Although you might not like it (especially if you're a high achiever who likes to excel in all areas), acknowledging it gives you the permission to better manage your time and energy so you don't burn out or get sick. Sometimes we can't do it all at the same time.

Once you've acknowledged what areas need to be less of a focus, you need to make the hard decisions that will align your energy and time to your priorities. Do you need to hire someone to paint your living room instead of you doing it with the time you don't have? Do you need to step down from the charity you're involved in as you really don't have the time right now? If you want to spend more time with your kids, can you hold off on going for a promotion at work that requires you to put in more face time?

Just because you're saying no to something right now, doesn't mean it can't be a yes later on. But you do need to ask yourself with every invitation, email, text or ask you receive, will it bring you closer to your dreams and priorities and if not, can you say no? Remember, by saying no, you're saying yes to you and your dreams.

Also, be sure to communicate your expectations of yourself and others. If you're operating at 20% versus 100% one day and you need your spouse to step up, share how you're feeling and ask for help. (Brené Brown has a great video on how her husband and her do this you might want to check out.)[18] If you're expecting more of someone on a certain day, let them know. When we don't communicate our expectations, we run the risk that others will have a different set of expectations and one of us will end up disappointed.

Focus on pleasing yourself, not others

How many of you have seen *Runaway Bride* with Julia Roberts and Richard Gere? If you have, I'm sure you'll remember the part where Julia's character admits she has no idea what type of eggs she likes because she has just always gone along with the type her partner likes. When is the last time you went along with someone rather than told them what you actually liked or wanted? How often do you "people please"?

Well this next part is simple: You are going to practise putting yourself at the top of your priority list for the next little while. You are going to focus on doing more of what brings you joy, and you're going to ditch any guilt that comes up with it.

The first step is to list all the pleasurable activities that you enjoy. If you can't think of any, that's OK. Let's think back to when you were a kid, what did you do for fun? What made you smile or laugh? And can you do some of that now? Is there something you've always wanted to try like an art class, kickboxing or guitar? Do you enjoy massages, getting your nails done or meeting a friend for a walk? Do you have a favourite playlist and how often do you listen to it? Do you like reading, writing or photography? Do you like listening to live music, going to an art show or watching a sporting event on TV? How about a nice hot bubble bath with no distractions?

Ideally, I'd love for you to list three to five things that bring you pleasure and I want you to start scheduling them in.

The second step is to take your priorities list, boundaries and new expectations for yourself and practise saying no to anything that doesn't align with them. Start by saying no to something small and work yourself up. Remember, you're choosing the most important priority–yourself.

Care less what others think

Want to hear something ironic? Years ago, I put this note in my phone as a reminder–"CLWOT," short for *care less what others think*. But why did I use the short form? In case someone saw it. Hilarious, right? But hey, this is a hard one to do so whatever steps you need to take you there, go for it. To be honest, I like how CLWOT sounds and to this day, I use it as a reminder to myself.

Caring too much about how we're perceived can cause us to stay in situations we otherwise might have left sooner. We might stay in a job we don't like for too long. We change jobs or companies only to find out it wasn't the right move but we're too embarrassed to admit it or we worry what hiring managers will think if we change jobs after only a few months. Or we stay in a relationship for too long with a partner, a friend or a boss. Or we keep working at getting someone's approval but it never seems to come.

Whether you're a leader, parent, spouse or caring friend, wanting people to like us is a very common desire.

And what happens when we fear not being liked?

We shy away from uncomfortable conversations or situations.

We don't speak up.

We pretend to be someone else.

But here's the thing—not everyone is going to like you and that's okay. In fact, as one of my clients once shared with me, one of her previous VPs used to say, "If there's *not one person* in the room who doesn't like you, you haven't done your job as a leader."

A leader's job is to make tough decisions, ask questions, and challenge the status quo.

A true friend or spouse will speak up, even when it's uncomfortable.

Just because you say or do something that isn't likable, doesn't mean *you're* not likable.

Just like when our kids act out—it's their *behaviour* that's not likable, not them.

You need to detach who you are from the behaviour. Your decision or comment may not be likable, but it doesn't make you unlikable. And sometimes you need to risk not being liked to do what is right.

Another big mistake we make when it comes to perception is comparing ourselves to others in completely different situations than ours. Have you ever sat around comparing yourself to a homeless person? Sure, you've probably walked by one and thought how blessed you are but when it comes to work, your personal life or your accomplishments, who do you compare yourself to, on average? Likely your peers, neighbours, or perhaps even the leaders or trailblazers in your industry.

In my case, a few of my closest friends are solo moms. I am constantly in awe of how they do it. At times, it does help me get over me feeling sorry for myself when I'm tired or overwhelmed. But you know what else comparing ourselves to people in different situations does? It undermines how we're feeling. If I'm constantly telling myself to suck it up and get over it because so and so has to do it on their own, I'm beating myself up for how I'm feeling instead of validating it.

For example, my father-in-law recently passed away from cancer and it was an extremely sad, exhausting and stressful time for our family, especially for my husband, his mom and his sister. My husband, being the incredible person he is, spent months driving to and from his parents' house, taking them to appointments, running errands and spending the night at their place or the hospital. While caring for his dad trumped everything else going on in our lives, it didn't mean the other things stopped or went away. We both still had to work to make money, our kids had all of their activities and while we lowered our expectations of ourselves a lot, meals still needed to be made, laundry had to be done and our house had to be cleaned. On top of it all, my parents, whom I would normally lean on for support, were travelling (celebrating their 50th wedding anniversary on the trip of a lifetime). So during those few months, I felt like a working single parent.

I was exhausted and then I felt pissed off at myself that I felt exhausted because I thought that I should be able to handle it all and push through. And why did I feel that way? Because I compared myself to solo parents. And yes, they're frigging amazing but they have also figured it out, and I'm sure if they had a sudden change in their circumstances and schedules, they would also feel exhausted.

We need to stop comparing ourselves to others…but we also need to stop comparing ourselves to ourselves. So often, we see the younger version of us through rose-coloured glasses. Meaning, we only remember the good stuff, not the bad. And we compare ourselves to this filtered, slimmer, shinier version. Who we were before kids, jobs, mortgages and aging parents. Hopefully your life is better now than before but yes, it could mean you also have more stress, less sleep and less energy. The truth is you're never going to be that person again and if you're constantly comparing yourself to the younger you, you're only burning mental calories that could be better spent elsewhere. It's time to take her off that pedestal.

Instead, focus on the present you—and all the great qualities and experiences you have and that you bring to the table. Own your fabulousness! Forget what others think about you and how you compare to them—it doesn't matter. You were created unique for a reason and now is your time to shine.

For those of you who are ready, and I mean really ready, it's time to ditch the 3 P's. Tell perfection, people-pleasing and perception to take a hike. Now, I'm not saying you should turn into an asshole—you can be super successful and still be a good person. It just means you're done playing small or being scared.

If you're worried about becoming a narcissist or egotistical, guess what, you won't. Just the fact that you have that concern tells me that you are a good human being who is not going to be a jerk. So set those fears aside and get out of your own way. It's time to break free amazing, brilliant, talented, resilient and courageous YOU!

Ask for what you want

In *What Holds Us Back*, we talked about how people are not mind readers and how we can't assume people know what you want. We have to step outside of our comfort zone to speak up and ask for what we want. We have to be more like Rob Lowe in the story he shared in his memoir *Stories I Only Tell My Friends*.

When Rob Lowe was 13 and not yet known, he wrote a letter to producer Aaron Spelling asking him for a job. Six months later, he got a letter back from Aaron inviting him to come see the studio as long as he had his parents' permission and called ahead. Aaron ended his letter by telling Rob that he could see him having his job one day. (Picture mind blown emoji.) Now, I don't know the details of what was in this letter but perhaps it was that a 13-year-old had the guts to write to a super successful TV producer and share his dream of working in show biz.

Years later, Rob joked that he never did have Aaron's job, but his star IS right next to Aaron's on the Hollywood Walk of Fame.

In my case, knowing I wasn't going to pursue my secret silly dreams of being a speaker and an author, I had my heart set on getting into a specialized university program that accepted only 65 students each year. The day the answer came, I knew I had gotten in by the size of the envelope. (I had already received a small envelope from another university with a short but sweet rejection letter.) Excitedly, I opened the envelope and read "Congratulations, you've been accepted into the Bachelor of Commerce program with a specialization in International Business."

My heart sank.

This was NOT the program I wanted. The program I wanted was the Bachelor of International Business Program with a mandatory 3rd year exchange to another country.

I had applied to the wrong program. I was mortified.

I hopped in the car and drove to my dad's office to tell him. He suggested I call the admissions office and see if they could do anything. They said I could send through some documents and switch my application to the other program but there were no guarantees.

What if I was too late?

What if I didn't get into my dream program?

I knew it had to happen.

So, I found out who the decision maker was at the university, I got their fax number (this was the year 2000 after all) and I wrote a letter explaining my situation, how I had made a huge mistake and why I was so passionate about the International Business program.

I also remember driving to the high school and freaking out to my guidance counsellor.

I don't remember any other details, nor how I ever found out I was accepted, but that following September, I showed up at Carleton University as a proud Bachelor of International Business student, made incredible friends while I was there and gained the experiences of a lifetime.

None of that would have happened if I didn't speak up and ask for what I wanted. Sometimes we make mistakes but that doesn't mean they can't be fixed. We may need to roll up our sleeves, admit our mistake and have the guts to still go after what we want.

Other times we disqualify ourselves from what we want before we even get a chance to go for it. For instance, how many of us didn't apply for a job after reading the qualification criteria because we couldn't check off every single criterion on the list? Or maybe you wanted to submit your short story into a contest but then told yourself you'd never get picked so why bother? Maybe you didn't try out for a team because you assumed everyone else would be better?

If you're nodding along to any of this, can I ask a big favour, please? Can you STOP disqualifying yourself? Someone actually gets paid to do that so why not let them do their job. Plus, sometimes it's things like your personality or charisma that land you opportunities, not what's written on LinkedIn or your resumé. Sometimes you just have the *je ne sais quoi* that people are looking for and if you don't let yourself have the opportunity, it may pass you by. If anything, I invite you to reach out and connect with people over coffee or Zoom to learn more about an opportunity before you decide you're not right for it.

The month after I left my corporate job, I started contacting speaker bureaus (agencies who help speakers get booked) to begin turning my dream of being a motivational speaker into a reality. I didn't contact the bureaus asking to be a part of their roster. No, I contacted them to find out what it would take to get on their list so I could start to build my experience and material.

Next thing you know, I got an email asking if I was available for a call with the founder of the Speakers Bureau of Canada. I said yes and nervously waited for my phone to ring. It was only a call for me to gather more information but because it was so close to my dream job, I was scared I was going to mess it up or that it would be so out of my league, it would take years to accomplish.

But that call changed everything.

I had a lovely discussion with the founder where he told me about their process, what they look for in speakers and what makes a great speaker. He also asked about my career journey and background. And because I had nothing to lose, I confidently shared how much I loved presenting to people and how well some of my corporate presentations went. But, I was also transparent in that this was always in partnership with other colleagues. I had never developed my own material to share publicly.

As the call drew to a close, the founder said he would like to add me to the roster and that he would email me the documents to complete. I was shocked. Me? The person who just admitted they had never done speaking in this manner before was being asked to become one of their speakers? Plus, he shared what my speaker fee would be and my jaw dropped. I felt honoured and thanked them, then immediately called my parents to share the news!

Sometimes what others see in us is hard for us to see in ourselves and that's why we need to go for things and not disqualify ourselves before we get our chance. (Remember the story of me being told I could be Prime Minister one day or Rob Lowe being told he could be Aaron Spelling?)

So, how do you go about speaking up and asking for what you want? By taking the following steps.

Make a wins list

We all think we have better memories than we actually do (yes, even you who swears your mind is a steel trap) so we need to get better at recording our accomplishments. That's why I like the Weekly Wins List—the list of all your wins for the week, big and small. And while you don't need to do this exercise now, it is something I'd encourage you to start doing weekly either on a Friday or Sunday. And folks, making this list is not your time to be shy or modest. I want you to write down every win. Every. Single. One. A client sent you a thank you note for a job well done. A direct report complimented you or your leadership style. You made your budget. You paid an invoice on time. You sent an email you'd been putting off. You called someone instead of texting them even though you hate talking on the phone. A leader smiled at you in the hallway and knew your name. You had an uncomfortable conversation and survived. You spoke up in a meeting. You stood up for yourself or your team. You finished a document on time. You nailed a presentation. It doesn't matter what it was, just write it down.

And while you're add it, make one for your personal life too. You were present with your kids at dinner, you went for a run, you made a home-cooked meal, you went to bed early, you helped a friend, you donated your time to a great cause, you finally cleaned out that one cupboard.

By focusing on all of the things going well in your life right now, big and small, you are reminding yourself of everything you've learned, overcome and succeeded at and this builds up the confidence to speak up and ask for more of what you want in life.

Find the right approach

Going back to my earlier point of how leaders have more work on their plates and are not mind readers, while you may be a super driven high-achiever and think your boss should assume everyone on your team wants a promotion, it's very possible that they don't. So what do you have to do? You guessed it: Ask for what you want. But, in the right way. If you go in prepared, you have a much higher chance of hearing yes.

For any of you parents reading this, kids are a great example of asking for what they want. They either do it in a way that pisses us off and gets a clear no (*"Mom, get me a snack now"* or *"All of my friends get to do it so I should too"*) or they do it in a super clever way that at least gets us to stop and contemplate a yes. My eldest is an expert at this–he spends time researching and building a case so that when he comes to me, he is factual and pulls on my heartstrings. For example, during the pandemic he wanted a bearded dragon (a.k.a. lizard). He did his research to find out how to take care of them and came to me with that information, plus he shared he was lonely and having a pet in his room would help him feel better. (Kids, take note–parents never want you to feel lonely.) He won his case.

When it comes to building a case for getting what you want, focus on facts over emotions. However, keep in mind what personality you're appealing to and leverage that too. If emotions will work with the person you're making the ask to, use them. But if that person is not an emotional person, stick to the facts.

Build your case with these three components: The ask, the proof points and the timeline, as shown in the the following examples.

Example 1: Asking for a promotion

1. **The ask**. This is where you state what you want (i.e., to be promoted to the next level). Keep it clear, concise and to the point. When we're nervous about asking for something, we have a tendency to have a long intro and go around the ask a few times before getting to it. But this can just cause confusion and take away from your case.

2. **Proof points**. Here you'll want three to five examples. If it's a promotion, have examples of your best work–think of these points as what you'd include in the results section of your resumé. Things like: exceeded revenue target by A%, reduced time to market by B%, received C award, improved efficiency in the process by D days, led E project to completion on time, improved employee engagement by F%, voluntary member of Committee G.

Basically, you're looking for anything that exceeds your base job description. That signals you're ready for the next level.

If your ask is a proposal to fix a challenge, come with three to five pain points/statistics that your solution will fix, what the solution is and the expected outcome.

3. **Timeline**. Propose a timeline you think is fair and feasible for your proposal.

Be sure to include your asks in your employee development plan. Don't just wait to bring it up during your annual review–bring it up during your 1:1s with your manager too. Remember, don't assume you'll get it based on how long you've been in your role or what your background is. You need to ask questions and understand what they're looking for and where they see you in that process. If you don't agree with the criteria or where they see you, you have a choice. Work to meet that criteria or find another job that's more aligned with what you want.

Example 2: Getting more help at home

The same principles work at home too. Let's say you're hoping your partner can help out more at home or with the kids. Take some time to think about your approach and how you can tailor it to best meet their communication style. Then make sure to be clear about your ask, come ready with proof points, and offer up a timeline to make it happen.

For example, let's say you'd like to have one night a week that's designated "you time." (One of my clients and her husband do this and I absolutely love it.) Here's what that could look like using the steps above.

1. **The ask.** Having one night a week where you don't pick the kids up, make dinner or lunches, clean, do baths or bedtime.

2. **The proof points.** By you having one night off, you'll be more rested and happier, making you more fun to be around for

everyone involved. If you're paying for a sitter, what's the return on investment for you taking time for yourself? Sure, it might cost you money but what are you getting in return–perhaps being more productive the other days, prioritizing your health, etc. Another proof point for any of you who suffer from guilt when it comes to your kids is looking at the example you're setting for them. By taking a night to yourself, you are showing them how important it is to make it on your list of priorities. That by taking care of yourself, you can show up stronger and better for other people.

3. **Timeline.** Propose when this new arrangement could start and the steps you can take to help make it happen. For example, showing your partner or sitter what they need to do when it comes to pick-ups, dinner, lunches, bedtime, etc. It might be painful teaching them the steps at first but just think of the time you'll get back from it.

Lastly, in any instance, personal or professional, always remember the golden question–*what's in it for them*? Remember, people are selfish and if you're asking them to help you, it will go a long way if you can give them reasons as to why this will benefit them (or if there are trade-offs you can discuss). If you're looking for a promotion, perhaps that will ease your current boss' workload or stress levels. If you're asking for a night of "me time," can your partner have the same on another night?

Regardless of what it is, take the time to build your case and then choose the right time to bring it up. If your boss is super stressed and behind on a deadline, wait. If your kids are running wild around the house and you and your partner are exhausted, wait. And if people need time to digest and think about what you proposed, let them. But don't be afraid to follow up too if you don't hear back from them in a timely manner, whatever your definition of timely is.

If you need help committing to making the ask so you don't back out, mention it in your email or text to the person you're making the ask to. You don't need to go into details but you could add something like:

"In our 1:1 on Wednesday, I'd love to talk about my career progression."

"Tonight after the kids are in bed, can we sit down and chat? I have some ideas for how we can feel more energized."

Then if you can, make the ask at the start of your chat. Otherwise, you'll be thinking about it the whole time and might back out.

Celebrate your wins

Earlier I had you keep track of your weekly wins and here I want to encourage you to celebrate them. All of them. I'm not saying to go buy yourself a present for each win but even just acknowledging your wins motivates you to focus on what is going well in your life and to keep going.

And don't wait for the big ones—celebrate each and every one, especially the small ones.

Celebrate making the ask.

Celebrate feeling uncomfortable.

Celebrate feeling prepared.

Celebrate the rejections because rejections mean you're putting yourself out there.

And when they come, because they surely will, celebrate the YES's!

Take the bloody risk

I'd love for you to take a moment and think of all of the times you've held yourself back in your life. This can be what you wrote down in *What Holds Us Back* or it can be new things.

When did you let BS, excuses or bad habits win?

What stories did you believe about yourself that caused you to say no to a great opportunity?

What are all of the things you didn't do out of fear: Fear of public speaking, fear of trying new foods, fear of meeting someone new on a blind date, fear of not being good enough.

Now think about these times and notice which ones still sting a little bit. What is it about them that stings? We can't change the past, nor do I want guilt hanging over you from missed opportunities. I'm sure saying no to many of these was the right call at that time. But I do want you to remember a bit of the sting-y sensation so that the next time one of the 3 P's or fear stops you from trying something new or risky, you remember how it feels to not do it and you decide to go for the ones that make sense to you.

When I was in Grade 11, I started taking Spanish classes at school and immediately fell in love with the language. (Thank you Señor Almeida for sparking that flame for me as I'm now fluent in Spanish.)

Coincidentally, I also had my first serious boyfriend that year and he happened to be in my Spanish class with me. One day Sr. Almeida handed out pamphlets for us to go to Costa Rica on a mini exchange. I was so excited to go until my boyfriend told me it was a horrible idea. Who knows if my parents would have let me go as I didn't even bring it up to them but it always stuck with me as one of those missed opportunities. My boyfriend told me it was a bad idea and I listened (hello, people pleasing).

Remembering this experience came in handy when in my second year of university, I started planning where I would do my exchange the following year. I had a choice between Mexico, Peru, Chile and Spain. This time, I decided that the only person I would talk to about it was the exchange coordinator at the school. I didn't want my then boyfriend, parents or friends weighing in when they wouldn't have as many details as the coordinator. As it turns out, I ended up picking Peru–perhaps the most dangerous of the four options at the time and the country where only one other student was going–so I could immerse myself in the culture and not hang out with only Canadians. This small town girl would be moving to Lima, Peru, a city of 10 million people for 10 months. Was it risky? Sure! I was nervous as hell. It also turned out to be one of the most rewarding things I ever did.

The thing is, taking risks still scares the crap out of me. But even though I get anxious, feel uncomfortable and have felt sick about it on many occasions, I don't let it stop me. And when I hear stories from the gurus I look up to, like Mel Robbins, and hear that they too can still get anxious, I know it's never going to go away. But, it might get easier.

I've taken a lot of risks–moving to new places, starting new jobs, ending relationships with people I loved but where I didn't see a future. What might feel super risky to someone else may not feel that way to you. The move to leave my six-figure salary and VP title in the corporate world to start my own coaching and speaking company did not feel risky to me, as crazy as that might sound. Perhaps because it was completely aligned with what I wanted to do and what I'd been working towards. Perhaps it's because I did the worst-case scenario planning and many of the worst cases were the same as if I tried a new job in a company and got let go. Or, perhaps it's because my husband shares in our expenses. I'm not sure how to explain it but it still throws me off when I have people tell me how courageous it was to go out on my own. Sure, it took bravery, but I think the more risks you take to figure out what you want in life, the easier it gets. At least, that's my personal take.

This became clear for me when I was walking my dog while listening to Jay Shetty's podcast episode where he interviewed Gretchen Rubin, a lawyer turned writer and happiness subject matter expert. Just a couple of minutes in and the following quote stopped me in my tracks and simultaneously brought a smile to my face and tears to my eyes. Here's what Gretchen said: "I would rather fail as a writer than succeed as a lawyer."[19] Wow. Finally I had words for these feelings I'd been carrying around with me for so long. I too would rather fail as a coach and entrepreneur than further succeed in the corporate world.

Getting back to being big, bold and brave–the mantra I have lived by since 2019–I have an assignment for all of you to complete this week. It might feel silly or uncomfortable but I don't really care because once you do it, it will make you feel proud and happy.

Ready?

Exercise: The Daring List

I want you to pick one thing from *The Daring List* below and do it this week. If I can take it one step further, I invite you to pick the thing that really feels like stepping outside of your comfort zone. If some of the items below feel like they're something you'd regularly do, skip them and try something you wouldn't. You'll notice there's a range of things here for that very reason.

Ok, here's the Daring List:

1. Write a letter or email to someone you admire but whom you don't know personally and send it to them. (The send part is key here.)

2. Have an uncomfortable conversation with someone you know. If you've been wanting a raise or promotion but haven't asked yet, do so. If you have been meaning to make amends with someone in your life, go for it. If you've wanted to ask someone out on a date, now is the time. If you've been putting off sharing how you feel with someone, do it now.

3. Go skinny dipping or finish your shower with cold water for one minute.

4. Write your eulogy, the speech someone close to you will give at your funeral. Be sure to include what you want to be remembered for.

5. Strike up a conversation with five strangers (and no, "How are you" doesn't count). Bonus points if you tell them you are an X (insert the future role you're working towards—for example, I am a writer, I am a guitar player, I am a team leader).

6. Sign up or apply for that job, program, class or opportunity you've been scared to commit to.

7. Share something vulnerable on social media.

8. Attend a networking event by yourself.

9. Ask someone you admire in your network to go for a coffee (virtual or in-person).

10. Take yourself on a date: Go to a restaurant, the movies, etc.–alone.

Ok, now I want you to write down which of the above you're going to do. (Remember, I want it to feel scary and uncomfortable for you. I want your hands to get sweaty and your heartbeat to quicken–that's how we'll know you're stepping outside of your comfort zone, the area where you grow.) Next write down when you're going to do it by and lastly, share it with someone who can vouch that you did it. If I can be that person, fantastic. Send me a message on Instagram @shannontalbot_coaching with your commitment statement. Then, once you've done it, share what you did but most importantly share how it made you feel.

For any of the above to feel truly successful, let go of any expectations you have. Expectations of how the conversation will go, of getting a reply, of getting what you want. Focus solely on doing the task and expecting nothing in return. Then, notice how that feels. How it feels to take action, be vulnerable, take risks. Note how you feel before and after taking action. How it feels to not focus on the outcome, since we can't control what happens.

Then, I want you to pick another item from the list and repeat the process the following week. Or do something not on the list but that scares you (as long as it doesn't put you in harm's way, please).

You got this!

If you're looking for inspiration for the Daring List that is completely unrelated to working or parenting–here's something I did in university that I still can't believe I did.

In my first year of university, a band called I Mother Earth (a Canadian rock band) played at my university. Well, let's just say I've always (and still do–shhhh, don't tell my husband) had a thing for musicians. So, when this band took the stage and I saw the guitarist with his spiky blue hair and alternative style, I crushed hard. Then I had the crazy idea that I just had to meet them. When the show finished, I grabbed my friends, and we walked around the venue at the school. Wouldn't you know, we came across their tour bus out back. And what does a wilder, younger Shannon do? Go right up and knock on the door, of course. They opened the door, I told them my friends and I thought they were awesome, and they invited us into their bus.

Hanging out in a bus was cool and all but it was also the biggest party night on campus that night, so we invited them to come with us to the bar. And guess, what? A few of them, including the cute guitarist, did and we had a night I'll always remember–*the night I partied with rock stars.* (Okay stars might be pushing it but this was the closest I'd ever gotten to meeting anyone famous and I was smitten!) It was a night of fun dancing and listening to music and staying up all night. (Get your heads out of the gutter, this was pure partying and nothing more.)

In fact, the next morning, when I got back to my dorm room still wearing my concert-going clothes and had to get ready for a math test at 8:30 a.m., I called my dad to tell him what I'd done and how we'd partied with rock stars all night. I still laugh thinking about this. My dad who doesn't drink, smoke or swear gets a phone call from his daughter at 8 a.m. telling him how she's so proud of knocking on that bus door and hanging out with stars. Either he was a great actor or he was genuinely happy for me, plus a little shocked I think.

Something else I did that night that was very out of the ordinary for me—I went out the night before a math test. Perhaps I felt less stressed as it was math, my least favourite subject, so not one I put as much pressure on myself for, but getting good grades was always important to me. And you know what happened? I scored 100% on my test. No joke, and math is also one of my weaker subjects.

Sometimes letting off steam and letting go of results can truly work, plus the adrenalin that comes from stepping outside your comfort zone can be extremely energizing. Thinking about how bold I was that night still puts a smile on my face.

So now, what's going to put a smile on your face? What's the risk you're going to take that's going to have you calling up someone to tell them that crazy thing you still can't believe you did? If you want to tell me, I'd love to hear it and cheer you on. Message me on Instagram @shannontalbot_coaching.

Trust your gut

The next strategy to break free is perhaps the one that requires the least amount of effort. It requires learning to trust your gut. As Ted Lasso says, *"Just listen to your gut, and on the way down to your gut, check in with your heart. Between those two things, they'll let you know what's what."* And yes, I used a quote from a fictional character as I just love Ted Lasso's character and how he's always staying true to himself.

Some of you may be great at trusting your gut already and some of you may have your 3 P's interfering and telling you why following your intuition is a bad idea. So here's a little story for you to show how our guts know more than they get credit for.

I'd like for you to take a moment and remember the start of the pandemic. I know it was a difficult and very trying time for many of you but I want you to think back to how much uncertainty there was basically overnight and the impact it had on you, your work and your family.

Now, I want you to picture having moved out of your house into a 700-square-foot condo with your husband and three children, all under the age of 8, while your house was being renovated. Oh, and let's add that you're about to start a new job at a brand new company while trying to balance being a mom, wife, teacher and daycare worker.

That is the story of what happened to Nora. I met Nora years ago at one of the banks we were both working at. She was the VP of Brand Marketing and only a few years older than me, she had risen the corporate ranks quickly, landing her first VP role in her early 30s. What I loved about Nora was that she seemed so down to earth and real. She was kind and intelligent. And she prioritized her family and friend time. I aspired to be a leader like her. Nora and I didn't stay in touch when I left the bank but when I reached out to interview her for this book, she graciously accepted. And the story I got from her was not the one I was expecting. It was even better.

Nora learned the hard way to trust your gut. She had a great role in a great company but there was a lot of change starting to happen and Nora figured it was time to make a move. She got offered a job in a different company and even though her gut told her it wasn't the right move, she took it. As Nora shares, this was the first time in her career where she didn't listen to her gut and fumbled as a result. She joined a company where everyone had been in the same role for years and where the role she got was not the role she signed up for. On Day 1 she knew she had made a mistake. And while juggling her three kids, including a one-year-old, in a small condo, she was also struggling to understand what was expected of her at the workplace. And she couldn't get a clear answer.

Unfortunately, Nora had a bully for a boss and was never able to figure it out. The result? She was let go. It was the first time Nora had ever experienced failure in her life. It was a massive blow to her ego. She felt ashamed and told herself stories like she'd never bounce back or be able to afford the renovation they were doing. And for the first time in her life, Nora felt depressed.

When I asked Nora how she overcame this setback, she shared these four pieces of advice:

1. Know that time heals everything.

2. Have a personal support system. Nora's mom, husband and friends were incredible at supporting her during this difficult time. To help her ease back into things, her husband invited her to pick just one small task to do every day, like unloading the dishwasher. That she could do, and it built her confidence back up. Her friends also helped her take her next job, which was a step back, going from a VP to a Senior Director, unlike the kinds of job changes she had made up to now, which usually involved a promotion and vertical move. This taught her that sometimes things are a good plan even if it's not what you initially pictured—you just may need some convincing. Plus, career paths aren't always going to be linear, especially for someone who rises young, and that's okay.

3. Get the human touch. Nora found that going back into the office a few days a week had been something she'd missed during the pandemic. Being an extrovert, Nora needed in-person human interaction to feel more energized and happier.

4. Trust your gut. Nora's gut had told her not to take that new job but she didn't listen. Now she knows for next time.

Although it was a step back, Nora's transitional job was in a "nice, normal organization with a young team that helped keep her youthful" while she waited to land her next role that would get her back on track to her career aspirations. After two years, Nora found that role. Now she's back to being a VP at an organization with an amazing culture, mission and role, and she feels more fulfilled knowing she's back on even ground.

Nora's parting words to me were to not rush into something new. As the saying goes, "Don't run away from something, run to something."

And be sure to trust your gut along the way. Looking back, Nora would have taken more time to find a role that better aligned with what she wanted instead of rushing into something, especially when there were red flags, however sometimes we need to make mistakes to come out wiser.

Exercise: Learning to Trust Your Gut

The exercise for this chapter is simple—**the next time you have a decision to make—check in with your gut, see what it says and follow it**. Then afterwards, see if it was the right decision.

Strut your stuff

Oh my gosh, you are on your way to soaring to new heights and I am so excited for you. But first, we have one more step and that step is to take all of your uniqueness and awesomeness and strut your stuff.

I know what some of you are thinking–I'm not ready. I need more time. I need more experience. Blah blah blah. Your excuses, fears and beliefs are showing up right on cue to taunt you and see if you're ready to apply what you've learned in this book. And guess what? You are more than ready! Want to know why? Because practically every person on this earth is feeling the exact same way as you–that they're not ready or good enough or smart enough. In fact, remember the stat from Dr. Joe Rubino that 85% of people worldwide struggle with self-esteem? That means that *only 1.5 people out of 10 DON'T struggle with self-esteem.* Now let's have some fun and imagine the 15% that don't struggle are the narcissists and egomaniacs of the world and we don't want to be like them anyway. If pretty much all decent people struggle with self-doubt, what sets successful people apart? They strut their stuff even when they don't feel confident. What looks confident to us may not feel confident to them.

A great example of this comes from one of my oldest and dearest friends' 40th birthday party a few years ago. It was on her farm 30 minutes outside of my hometown on a gorgeous evening. The party started with a delicious buffet dinner followed by an epic dance party.

I didn't know a ton of people as I moved away from the area when I was 18, but that was OK–if there are great tunes and a dance floor, I'm good to dance the night away. While dancing, I was admiring one woman–her style, her dance moves–she seemed so authentic and confident and I was in awe. Later that week I had a call with my therapist where I shared this story saying how I desired to be more of my authentic self, like that woman was in a crowd of people. My therapist stopped me and asked me how I knew she was being her authentic self. I answered, "Because she was so confident." To which she asked me, "But do you know if she felt confident, or could she have been acting confident?" A lightbulb went off for me–I didn't know. No one could know except her.

So here's the one thing I know to be true about confidence–we never truly know how confident someone feels unless they tell us and going around sharing when we're not feeling confident isn't something we generally do, especially in certain situations like work. Nor do we always want to know when someone isn't feeling confident. For example, no one wants to see their doctor showing self-doubt when heading into surgery, right? The same can be said for having a new leader. While self-doubt can be endearing at times, it can also make people weary if the leader doesn't seem confident in her abilities.

While it's great to understand where our self-doubt comes from (i.e., all of the things we talked about in *What Holds Us Back* that's had a negative impact on us), the truth is it doesn't really matter at the end of the day. What's important is that you don't let your lack of self-confidence stand in the way of overcoming what holds you back to break free.

The other truth bomb I have to drop on you is this–there is no specific five-step model or silver bullet to build your confidence. A lot of the exercises you've done throughout this book are already helping your confidence grow (especially repeating the new positive stories to yourself daily). The real secrets to confidence are a) practice and b) understanding what a realistic definition of success is.

Practice ~~makes perfect~~ builds confidence

As we talked about in the 3 P's, unless you're working in a life-or-death industry, perfection is not what we are striving for. We're striving for done or good enough. And how do you get to that? Why practice, of course. And consistency.

I know you're well aware of the examples I'm about to give where practice is the only way to get better but this is a point I really want you to remember. Because somehow as we get older, we assume we should know how to do stuff–especially in the work environment.

So let's take a trip down memory lane and look at some of the things you likely had to practise, regularly. I'm guessing you made many mistakes along the way which in fact helped your progress. Things like:

- Walking
- Talking
- Biking
- Swimming
- Writing
- Reading
- Driving
- Cooking

Right? Would you disagree with me on any of the above? Was studying for your written driver's test enough for you to learn how to drive? No. You had to get behind the wheel and actually do it.

Let's look at some more skills:

- Developing a presentation or proposal
- Creating a financial budget
- Learning a new software program or app

- Public speaking

- Managing people

- Conducting a performance review

- Receiving feedback

- Giving feedback

- Having uncomfortable conversations

- Reading someone's body language or tone

- Writing a cover letter or resumé

- Interviewing

- Leading a project

- Leading a meeting

- Being in a relationship

- Kissing

- Owning a pet

- Parenting

- Hosting a party

- Planning an event

How many of these were you awesome at the first time you tried them? Surely, you got better at each of these with practice. Well, while some skills are easier than others and some people are naturally better at some things, the bottom line is that we all had to learn and practise each skill that we have.

We have to look at confidence the same way we'd look at any skill, as something that requires consistent practice. By doing the things that make you nervous and uncomfortable, the things that your brain tells you not to do because it wants to keep you safe, we build confidence. You have to pull out all the ways to overcome your obstacles, including even the magical question—what is the worst that can happen when I do this? Do it anyway. And that's how you get good, and confident, at anything.

Success is in the definition

Sometimes our lack of confidence is because something is brand new and scary and sometimes it's because we don't feel successful. And that could be because you use your parents' or society's definition of success. Remember my Game of Life story at the start? Go to university, be a lawyer, get married, get a house, and have four kids? Or my client who wanted to "know everything and everyone in her industry"? This definition alone was setting her up for failure and do we feel confident when we fail? Not likely.

And what happens if that definition of success doesn't light you up? Or if you define success by your title or how much money you make and then you find yourself making less money, either due to uncontrollable circumstances such as job loss or a deliberate job change to have more work-life balance or less stress or more joy?

Have you ever stepped back and thought of what *your* definition of success is? How would you define it for where you are in your life right now? And how might it change as you hit each new milestone in your life? Be sure to think of all aspects: money, title, responsibilities, how you spend time with family and friends, what relationships you have and their importance, what you do for fun, hobbies, work-life balance, etc.

Let's imagine for a moment you're making really good money but burning out in the process. Sure, you can buy nice things but perhaps you spend many evenings, weekends and vacations working. You might enjoy your work, the challenge and the people, but the hours and the responsibility are killing you. You're constantly multi-tasking and wishing you had a nine-to-five job where you could close your laptop at the end of the day, go home and spend quality time with your family, fit in a workout and a show with your partner and not think about work until the next day when your workday begins and you open your laptop again.

Or what if you pursue that dream career of yours, the one you've thought of since you were a little kid, but in taking it, you get a 30% pay cut? Will you be happy?

The answer can be YES if you let it. But it takes some pre-work. Some pre-work I wish I had done before chasing my dream. You have to define what success looks and feels like to you. Make sure it aligns with your desired role, lifestyle and idea of work-life balance.

A lot of the time, this means redefining how you view success, especially as pertains to money and titles.

I learned both of these the hard way.

Earlier in the book, I shared how one job change I had meant I went down in title but up in salary. At first, I thought, who cares what my title is as long as I'm making more money, right? Wrong! No one knew how much I was making, but what they could see was my title change, and what I started to fear was what others would think. "Wow, Shannon went from a Director to a Senior Manager. Could she not hack it as a Director?" It sounds harsh and maybe some people did think that but at the same time, lots of companies have lots of different titles and levels so no one can truly know unless they've worked at both places, but still, I felt like a failure. I had tied my definition of success to be at a certain level by a certain age. I got that and then when I changed jobs, I felt like I moved backwards down the ladder and with it went my self-confidence.

At the time I didn't realize what that shift did to me nor did I redefine my version of success. I didn't look at it as success now meant I could eat dinners with my family and take the kids to play dates and activities on the weekend. If I had rewritten my definition and added these in, I would have felt like a star, not a failure. I also didn't stop and think about what lit me up professionally, otherwise, I likely would have waited for another job to come along that better aligned with my values and priorities (like Nora's story earlier of running to something, not away from something).

Sometimes we need to remind ourselves why making a change is good for us, especially when it's not something we originally planned. And we need to tell our ego to step aside.

The next time this happened was more recent. I was making an incredible salary, with the VP title I'd worked really hard for (the next logical step after being a Director), but I knew it was time to chase my dreams of being an entrepreneur. I saved six months' worth of my salary, tested out my coaching business on the side, gave six weeks' notice at work so I wasn't leaving them in a bind and left my corporate job.

My parents were the proudest I'd seen them. My kids loved that I was now able to walk them to and from school, and my husband was happier knowing I was finally going after what I wanted in my career. (I'm sure he didn't mind that I was able to help out more around the house either.) My happiness was contagious, and it felt incredible. People kept telling me how courageous I was for taking the leap into entrepreneurship, but for me, it just felt like I had finally found what lit me up and I had to live it.

A few months in, I had everything I had worked my butt off for and...I felt like crap more days than not. Why? Because yet again my definition of success hadn't been updated to account for my massive job and lifestyle change. For me, being successful traditionally meant making great money. Sure, I now had the title of Founder & CEO but come on, I'm a company of one, so that no longer meant much. As for my salary? It was peanuts compared to what I used to make. My first full year in the business resulted in me making 25% of what I'd made the previous year in the corporate world.

Looking back, I could have looked at the statistics that 20% of small businesses fail in the first year.[20] I could have felt proud knowing every dollar I made was a result of blood, sweat and tears, and that having never done business development before, I did a phenomenal job. Or that in just a few months of starting my business, I'd developed not one but two revenue streams: coaching and speaking.

But I didn't look at those things. I only looked at my income and how much debt I was taking on and I felt like crap. I felt like I had failed. It wasn't until talking to my cousin's wife who was also starting her own business that I realized I had set completely unrealistic goals. Because I had six months' of savings, I had set a goal to make a high monthly income just six months in. In hindsight, that was ridiculous. Most new businesses do not make a profit in the first year and I'd set out to not only make a profit but to also make a BIG profit. And what happens when we make unrealistic goals or definitions of success? We set ourselves up for disappointment. We feel like failures.

We can only ever control our actions, not our results or outcomes.

I had to write a new definition of success that encompassed all the reasons why I started my own business. I wrote:

I am a successful entrepreneur who helps people live happier, healthier and more fulfilling lives. I have a great work-life balance so I can walk my kids to and from school some days, attend their extracurricular activities and spend quality time with my hubby. I get to choose my clients and whether I spend any evenings or weekends working. I am financially stable and I'm great at sticking to a budget. We are part of an incredible community with two-way love, support and fun.

I also have a dream where I do include a financial target but the difference is it's a stretch goal and not how I define success. My new definition of success includes things within my control that are attainable and realistic. And my stretch goal is a driving force to remind me that the only way to continue to chase my dreams is to do things even when I don't feel confident.

Have you ever thought about what your confidence is tied to? Your looks, achievements, status, money, relationships? And what happens if any of those things goes away or changes over time? How can you start loving yourself for you and all the incredible things you already are, do and have inside you?

My next exercises will help you do just that.

Exercise: Writing Your Definition of Success

When you are lying on your deathbed, what will you look back on with pride? What are the key things that stand out that tell you whether or not you were successful?

It's OK if they have a title or money associated with them. If that's important to you, by all means, include them. But make sure you aren't only defined by your role or external circumstances as it can be hard to create and stick to boundaries at work or to prioritize your well-being or relationships when your definition of success centres around work or money. Results and external circumstances like job titles and money are also largely out of our control and can change in an instant.

What is in your control are your attitude, habits, boundaries, choices, expectations, behaviour, priorities and values. The more your definition of success can revolve around those key elements, the more satisfied, content and fulfilled you will feel.

Exercise: Create Your Triumph Tales

Your Triumph Tales is a list of every single thing you've done, achieved, overcome or accomplished in your life. Note that this is different from your "Weekly Wins" because, for your triumphs, you're going to go back to when you were a child to start the list whereas the weekly wins only look at the past seven days.

I don't care how big or small the thing is, you're going to include it on your list. It's going to start out a bit silly. You're going to include things like "I learned to walk, talk, ride a bike, cook, do laundry, write, use a laptop, use a phone," etc. (Remember that list of things above that we had to learn and practise?) Then you're going to look at all of the projects you've worked on, any hobbies or sports you've learned, any awards or achievements you've earned, all of the jobs you had, your accomplishments from them, the relationships you started, nurtured and/or ended (bad bosses, toxic culture, negative colleagues), the pets or humans you've raised, as well as any difficulties or events you survived or overcame.

Next I want you to **put a reminder in your calendar to review your Triumph Tales list every Monday morning before you start your week**. Yes, it might seem silly or feel like you're bragging but really you're strutting yourself *for you*. You're reminding yourself you can do hard things and overcome challenges. That you're more capable than you give yourself credit for. That you have unique experiences that make up the awesome person you are today.

On the hard days, you're going to pull out this list to remind yourself how incredible you are. That the world needs you and your gifts and when you break free, you are doing the world a favour. That you will be in a better place because you are living in alignment with what you value and believe.

And you're going to use this confidence, belief and pride to keep dreaming and keep going.

You are going to soar to new heights. You are going to do things so many don't because they don't overcome what holds them back. You are courageous and you have the tools, awareness and insight to set yourself free. You are ready to turn your dreams into reality.

WHAT KEEPS US GOING

"Success means having the courage, the determination, and the will to become the person you believe you were meant to be."

–George Sheehan,
American physician and author

You are on your journey to break free and soar to new heights. Your beautiful vision awaits and all that's missing is for you to continue to show up and live in it every day.

But in order to keep our dreams alive, we have to be realistic and remember what Dr. Stutz said about pain, uncertainty and constant work never going away. So many people reach their dreams but then ditch all their efforts as soon as they hit a new bump in the road. They think that the hard work is done and they can just coast from here on out. So if you start to find yourself in that situation, I want you to picture me playing that game show buzzer indicating "wrong answer" very obnoxiously so that you come back to reality and remember this lesson.

It is a fact that life will throw us curve balls and sometimes, just when everything is going right and on track, we get hit with one. Things like being so successful you forget how to prioritize your well-being and you head towards burnout. Or you receive some feedback that is a hit to your self-confidence. Or you lose your dream job.

The good news is this book has prepared you to handle those curve balls like a pro. Depending on what the new obstacle is, you can go back to *What Sets Us Free* and use the exercises that will best help you. It might mean setting new priorities and boundaries, writing new stories or reminding yourself of all of your awesomeness. It might also mean pushing back against those bad habits that tend to sneak up when we're not at our best.

While we've covered the main tools and strategies you need to break free, here are a few extras to help you keep going and deal with those curve balls.

Do the work

We all know those people. The ones who talk a big game, yet rarely follow through.

The ones who have brilliant ideas that get you super stoked but then always have an excuse as to why now is not the right time to actually implement them. Or that once they have the money it will happen. Or once things settle down. But they never actually take action on it.

Do you have someone in your mind right now? And did they ever follow through?

Unfortunately, it can take a while to realize the people who are all talk and no action but once you do, I hope you realize changing this behavior in someone else is really hard.

Sometimes it's due to fear or sometimes it's laziness, but a lot of time these people enjoy the ideating but not the execution.

Like the friend who keeps having incredible business ideas but fears failure so never tests them out.

Or the boss who keeps promising you a promotion but is afraid to have the difficult conversations to make it happen.

Or the partner who promises the stars and the moon but fears commitment and can't bear the thought of truly settling down.

The good news is you are already ahead of the pack by putting the time, effort and energy into reading this book and doing the exercises. You're already taking action and doing the hard work whether you realize it or not! You have your dream, you have faced your obstacles and are on your way to setting yourself free. You, my friend, are already going places.

Fortunately or unfortunately, the ones who choose to free themselves aren't as common as we think. Therefore once we do, we can go on to be pretty freaking amazing.

Some might say taking action is the hardest part, but I prefer to look at it as exciting. You've done the groundwork, you've laid the foundation and now, it's time to act.

And for any of you sitting there wondering if now is the right time, know that it is! Perhaps you're thinking you should wait a bit until things quiet down at work, or until your kids get older or until you feel happier with your life. There's that dreaded "should" again. The thing about life is as soon as one project or busy time ends, a new one quickly follows. There is never the perfect time. There is only now.

How we get started with chasing our dreams is the same way we get started with anything. By taking it one step at a time.

And if you're not sold yet, here's a pretty compelling stat for you. If you work on getting better by just 1% every single day for a year, you'll end up 37x better by the end of the year.[21] Not too shabby!

So how do you do that? Read on.

Be consistent

Consistency is what elite athletes, actors and the great business leaders of the world have in common. They're consistent in what they say *and* do.

They're consistent in:

- Setting intentions
- Showing up
- Doing the work
- Being open to learning
- Applying their learnings
- NOT letting setbacks, failures or fear hold them back

What steps can you take towards your vision and be consistent with? Think of it as if you were training for a 10-kilometre run. It's likely that you're not going to go from never running to running 10 kilometres overnight. You're going to start training by going for a shorter run at first and then gradually building your way up. The same is true with chasing our dreams. What habits require consistency for you to get there? Perhaps you need some habits to boost your energy? Protect your time? Give you the freedom to spark creativity? Do you need to read or study for a certain amount of time every day or week? Do you need consistent practice with speaking up? Whatever it is, consistency is the magic ingredient.

The thing about consistency is it seems boring. We gravitate to stories where someone became a sensation overnight. We want the same but rarely is that the case. Rarely do we watch someone practising every day to get 1% better.

That's why I love stories like soccer legend Lionel Messi. In fact, we have a poster with his picture and the below quote on my eight-year-old's wall—a saying he reads before going to bed each night.

"I start early and I stay late, day after day, year after year. It took me 17 years and 114 days to become an overnight success."–Lionel Messi

While consistency seems boring, it's what we want in people. We want people to be consistent in their actions and behaviours (well, the good ones). We want to able to count on them or know they'll follow through when they say they will. Consistency is what gets you to that 37x improvement.

Keep what lights you up close

In addition to being consistent, keep what lights you up–that beautiful vision you created at the start of the book–close to motivate and get you through the hard days.

Think of a house reno. Whether you've lived through one or watched one on TV, I want you to picture how it starts: With a vision. You know what the end result is going to be: that beautiful, new custom design. You also know how much it's going to cost you, approximately. It's exciting even if it's costing you a lot.

Then what happens? You have to set up a tiny kitchen in your living room, move into your basement for a few weeks or perhaps move out of your house into a rental that just doesn't feel like home. But, you're willing to do it as the end result is worth it.

So, you're making the best of your situation and you get a call from your contractor. You find out the wall you wanted moved can't be moved because it's load bearing, or the countertop you want is 30% more money than you anticipated, or they found an issue inside the walls that will now take away from your budget. Do you give up on the reno? Not likely. You make compromises. You come to terms with the realization that it's not going to be exactly as you pictured it. You might be upset for a few days or angry with your contractor, but you know in the long run, it's still going to be better than when it started.

And that's the end goal. *Have something be better than when it started.*

House renovations are messy, frustrating, time-consuming and costly. Yet over 50% of homeowners will do one or two major projects in a year[22] and endure the headaches, knowing the result will be beautiful.

Human transformation is the same. It's also messy, frustrating, time-consuming and can be costly. But if your end goal is to achieve your vision of what lights you up, then the work is worth the effort. Keep that vision front and centre to help you get through the setbacks.

Be okay with getting messy

When it comes to personal and professional development, so many people give up when things get messy. They give up right before their big break or breakthrough. Or they fail on the path they set out on and rather than tweak their path or find a new route, they choose to abandon their dreams altogether.

When my husband and I set out to be parents, we started the same way any couple would–OK, I'm not going to be *that* graphic but yes, you get the picture, we worked on trying to get pregnant. After a year of not getting pregnant, we set out on the second path–going to a fertility clinic. After a year of that not working, we set out on the third path–adoption.

Had we chosen to abandon our dreams of becoming parents after not getting pregnant, I wouldn't have achieved my dream of becoming a mom. Oddly enough, I had never dreamt of being pregnant or giving birth. Being blood-related to my children was not something that was important to me. I just wanted someone to love and nurture and how that happened didn't matter. Looking back now, I wouldn't have it any other way. My sons are phenomenal, and we have their incredible birth families as part of our larger circle that we see every year. Sure, it's a unique family model but it works for us and we love it.

So here's the thing. You might fail on your path. It might take a few attempts. The important thing is to keep going! Get back on your horse and remember how important your end goal is to you. And why not start celebrating the messy? Like calling a friend to let them know,

"Hey I feel super down and crappy and I think I'm failing at life but guess what, that's a sign I am transforming. I am on my way, baby!"

While you're at it, stop idealizing the process. Hard work is not always going to be fun. That's definitely one thing I learned from interviewing the fabulous Julie Cole, co-founder of Mabel's Labels, mom of six and recovering lawyer (a title she gives herself, which I love).

Her story starts in 2003 when Julie was pregnant with her fourth child and her oldest was diagnosed with autism. Realizing he was going to need additional support, she left her job as a lawyer to be home more. She then went on to co-found a start-up after noticing a gap in the marketplace: Labels for kids clothing and belongings that wouldn't come off in the washing machine or dishwasher. Fixing it meant making and testing labels late at night with three other women—her sister and two friends—in Julie's sister's basement. (Side note: Julie's advice to anyone wanting to start a new business? Find something that pisses you off and fix it.)

At the time, there wasn't social media to grow your business so they had to create awareness in the marketplace and spread the word through blogging, conferences, traditional media and word-of-mouth. Their efforts paid off and five years ago, they sold Mabel's Labels to Avery for $12 million.

Sounds like a dream come true, right? Totally, but to get there meant a lot of hard work and managing expectations with her family about why she was working evenings. She also had to have realistic expectations of her team, and Julie and her co-founders had to learn each other's communication styles so they could ensure that they were dividing the work evenly and talking openly. Julie did all of this while changing diapers for 12 years, 3 months and 28 days. A stat that made me smile when she shared it with me.

As Julie shared, entrepreneurship and motherhood are lonely and yet are often romanticized, which paints an unrealistic picture. In her case, her business of making labels looked a lot like making labels in the basement of a house until 2 a.m. each night.

It also means learning from your mistakes along the way. An early mistake at Mabel's Labels was holding on to people who were not a fit for the company for far too long, which is a waste of the company's money, the employees' time and impacts company morale!

In the early days, when team members were not a fit and did not align with the company's values, they avoided exiting them. They would do performance improvement plans, have conversations with them, give them too many chances.

They chose to avoid doing the uncomfortable over doing what was right. Like Julie says, "When you have to fire someone, it is awful. You will never feel good about it. But sometimes it has to get done. Getting the right people on and off your bus is key to a successful business and a good company culture."

In addition to the above, the last words of wisdom Julie gave me to share with all of you are gold:

1. When you chase your dreams, other people may not understand or support your decision, so you have to give up caring what they think of you. (Remember quitting the "P" in perception?)

2. The people you meet and skills you gain throughout your journey will be invaluable even if you don't recognize it at the time.

So, choose the actions you can be consistent with that will get you on your way, keep your exciting vision close and know that when things feel messy, it's a sure sign you are on your way! And if you fall, which you likely will, take the lesson, dust yourself off and get back up. You're getting closer with every step.

Embrace the journey

Trying to become a mom was one of the lowest times in my life.

During this time, I had many down days of lying in my bed watching TV, feeling sorry for myself. But I also did one thing that helped me get through my journey. I started a blog called What to Expect When You're *Not* Expecting. It was a way for me to process my feelings and to give myself hope that our journey would have a happy ending. Plus, I wanted to give others hope too.

Part of that journey included reminding myself of all of the things I should enjoy before having kids. So often we get so wrapped up in what isn't going right in our lives or working so hard towards a goal that we get tunnel vision and forget to enjoy the present. And if we can't enjoy the present, what's the point of creating a fulfilling life? So I posted a question on Twitter asking people what I should be sure to enjoy now. And here's what they came back with:

- Sleep in and sleep lots–I heard this one A LOT!

- Go out for dinner

- Travel

- Get the MBA

- Learn to cook

- Do a marathon

- Spend time with hubby and friends

- Read success stories

- Document the journey

- Be an advocate for adoption

Years later, this list became helpful when I embarked on my journey to entrepreneurship after identifying what it was that lit me up. Somehow I had the self-awareness to know the journey wasn't going to be an easy one so I took the above list and created a new one as a reminder to have patience in my self-discovery and career journey and still enjoy the ride.

I wrote down things like:

- Spend time with family/friends.

- Take the vacation!

- Don't take the first opportunity that comes along unless it's the right fit.

- Do self-discovery exercises—work with a coach, read books to help you grow, and reflect on your past and where you want to go.

- Make those to-do lists and enjoy checking off the most tedious tasks. Take each task as it comes and be proud of yourself for what you accomplish. Focus on the accomplishments, instead of the "outstandings"—the items still to do on your list.

- Focus on your own journey.

- Document your journey. Your struggles might help people later on.

- Embrace the journey and all the ups and downs that come with it.

Sometimes it's the unexpected experiences or moments we have on our journey that may be what we remember or cherish the most.

That's definitely what happened to me while living in Lima, Peru, in 2003.

A benefit to living in Peru was getting to enjoy its beautiful and diverse physical geography. Beaches, mountains, deserts and rainforests to explore meant many weekend trips with other fellow exchange students. Plus, travelling by bus was extremely economical and the list of places to visit seemed endless.

One trip I made a few times was to the northern part of Peru, to the beaches of Máncora. When it was gloomy and damp in Lima in the wintertime, it was hot and sunny in Máncora and quite inexpensive to visit. My friends and I would hop on the overnight bus Wednesday after class and 16 hours later we would arrive in Máncora. It was a bit crazy now that I think about it but for a 21-year-old student, it was awesome.

One of these trips, however, proved to be a bit more of an adventure. One that had my mom wanting to fly me home, immediately.

There were five of us on the bus back to Lima after a few fantastic days of sun, sand and surf. A few hours outside of Lima we awoke to find that our bus had stopped. When we went to ask our driver what was happening, he explained that there was a national strike in Peru, and the only highway to Lima was blocked. After waiting and seeing no movement, we were told we could get off and walk a few kilometres to the next town where buses were running. So we started out. Well, a few kilometres turned into TWO FULL DAYS of walking, with a stop in the middle to find somewhere safe to sleep before nightfall when it would become dangerous to be out in the desert due to theft. Oh, and since we'd been planning to be only at the beach, all I had were my sandals and one of mine broke just a few minutes in. Funny now but not so much at the time.

It was a bit scary not knowing if we'd be robbed or how far we would have to walk, yet it also meant having an experience unlike any other. We paid money to get doubled by kids on bikes, rode in wagons that should never carry people and were part of a large entourage making the trek. We also made it into the front section of the Lima newspaper–equivalent to Canada's *Globe and Mail*. The photographer who took the picture was the only driver we saw during our time and the picture reveals my look of disgust when he told us he wouldn't give us a ride! Little did I know he was taking this photo to highlight the national strike for the newspaper and that it would later help our teachers believe our story for missing class. Plus, it would forever be a memento of this crazy, unexpected adventure.

Another Peruvian adventure was when my brother Colin visited me from British Columbia. We signed up with a tour company to hike the Inca Trail over two days, a famous trek that takes you by foot to the ancient Inca ruins, Machu Picchu, outside of Cuzco, Peru. But the day before our trip, we were notified that the trek was cancelled due to a soccer match. Of course!

Our trek getting cancelled wasn't going to deter us from seeing Machu Picchu, one of the seven wonders of the world. Instead we took the train, stayed in a hotel near the ruins, then got up at 4 a.m. the next day to grab one of the first buses to be at the ruins in time for the sunrise (supposedly a spectacular sight). Only when we woke up, it was raining–a total downpour. Just like doing the trek, the chance of a sunrise was gone. We decided to head out early to the ruins anyway, hopped on the bus to the ruins and once there saw we could hike up to the top of Huayna Picchu–the mountain you see in the background of all the pictures showing Machu Picchu located behind the ruins. We passed only two other people on the trail, likely due to the slippery and steep terrain. It felt like we were forging our own path.

Hiking the trail was difficult, but we made it to the top of the mountain, sweaty and out of breath. We sat down and took in the view, proud of what we accomplished. Moments later, the rain clouds parted, and the magnificent ruins were revealed in their entirety, beautifully and dramatically.

It was a moment I'll never forget. And yet, had we arrived at the ruins on foot via the Inca trail instead of the bus, this moment likely wouldn't have happened as we would have been too tired to then climb this mountain with the million-dollar view.

In fact, a lot of my life has not gone according to plan and has turned out better than I ever could have imagined.

Sometimes, we just need to embrace the journey. We need to find ways to enjoy the everyday and find fun in the small moments.

Sometimes we just need to remember that everything might work out anyway—perhaps even better than you expected.

Along the way, we need to have patience that everything will turn out exactly the way it's supposed to.

Believe

Ok, I'm going to talk about Ted Lasso one more time–the Apple TV show where Jason Sudeikis plays the most incredible soccer (sorry, "football") coach ever and is probably the most authentic and inspiring leader I've seen as a fictional character on TV. (He has also become my other crush right now–don't worry, Chris knows about this one.)

Well early on in the series Ted puts a sign on the locker room door that says *BELIEVE*. And that he does. He believes in himself and others, which just always has you rooting for him to win.

And now I want you to believe.

Believe in your dreams.

Believe in your capabilities and skills.

Believe in yourself.

You may not be there yet, but if you don't believe you can get there, you're going to be fighting one hell of an uphill battle.

So, let's practise, shall we?

I want you to load up your dream one last time and I want you to start making "I" statements about your vision.

I am a ______________.

I am a runner.

I am an author.

I am a CEO.

These are all statements I've made about myself to other people long before they were actually true, when they were still just made of vision and dreams.

In fact, while writing this book I went to a quaint town outside of Niagara Falls called Niagara-on-the-Lake where I stayed at a romantic inn by myself and wrote my butt off. I wanted a nice quiet, pretty place and this spot was perfect. They also had a complimentary wine and cheese both days I was there. I told myself I wouldn't go to it–I was there for work. But it was free and who can pass up free stuff, right? So, I told myself I'd go down for one glass and some nibbles for a break, then come back up and write until dinner.

Well then I met Alyson, the lovely hostess at the inn, and she brightened my day. We started chatting and when she asked what I was doing there, I told her "I'm an author and I'm writing a book." She immediately asked me if she would know me and if she should get my autograph. I laughed, told her "Not yet" and answered the questions she had for me.

Later when I got on the elevator, a lovely couple who were also at the wine and cheese stopped me and said, "We overheard that you're an author–what's your book about?" And the following day during the next wine and cheese, I had another couple ask me what I was doing there and they also asked if they should get my autograph when I shared that I was an author.

Now here's the ironic thing. I used to get hung up on whether I was a writer or an author and I decided that being an author means having a published book. So when I was asked what I do, it took me a moment of internal dialogue to decide how I wanted to answer the question. In the end, I decided to answer that I was an author because I am on my way to being one. I have a strong belief in myself that this book will get published and that I'll write more after that. My belief isn't tied to being a best-selling author or making tons of money from my book but rather that I'm following my dreams of wanting to help people live happier, healthier and more fulfilling lives and this is one of the ways I do that. And by saying it out loud, it cements my vision and has me believing this dream is coming true. We don't have to have accomplished the thing to have belief in ourselves. We can believe in ourselves before it even comes true—in fact, it's that belief that will carry us there.

I want you to believe in whatever vision you have for yourself.

Picture it.

Feel it.

Believe it.

Write down those 10 Feels daily. Look at your vision board weekly. Identify and overcome new obstacles as they come up. Continue to set yourself free and keep going. With belief and action, your dreams will come true.

The only time it's too late is when you're dead

I have one more ask of you—I want you to take any preconceived notions that by age X you'd be doing Y and throw them out the window. When things come together and happen is only partially in our control—the rest comes down to timing and luck. At the end of your life, I want you to look back and be proud that you had the courage to create and live your dream life, whatever that looks like for you and however long it took to manifest. Because at the end I don't want you to have regrets like the ones palliative care worker Bronnie Ware outlines in her book, *Top Five Regrets of the Dying*.

Like the people who wished they'd…

- Had the courage to live a life more true to themselves rather than the life others expected of them.

- Hadn't worked so hard.

- Had the courage to express their feelings.

- Stayed in touch with their friends.

- Let themselves be happier.

Isn't not having regrets on your deathbed a pretty good motivator to chase your happy?

Leslie, one of my first clients, is a stellar example of not living with regrets and I was so happy when she agreed to let me share her story with all of you.

Since Leslie was six years old she wanted to be a veterinarian. She went to university for Health Sciences and in her third year she started panicking that she wouldn't get into vet school as you needed a +98% to get in and a lot of animal experience. Plus, there are only three vet schools in Canada, making it darn near impossible to get in.

Knowing her chances to get in were unlikely, Leslie didn't apply to vet schools. She chose Health Law instead and felt a lot of the pressure lift. But after her first year of law, she knew this wasn't what she was interested in. Like so many people who stay with things that don't interest them, Leslie stuck with it and articled at Trillium Health Centre. Once she graduated, she found herself following many of her classmates to work in a corporate law firm on Bay Street (the Wall Street of Canada). While she liked the people, the work and long hours were not her thing.

So, Leslie moved to a home health care company where she didn't practise law but acted as a liaison between outside legal counsel and the company. She didn't feel super fulfilled, but felt it was a better fit for her next goal—becoming a mom. Still, the what ifs of being a vet hung over her. And it took a tragedy for Leslie to finally pursue being a vet.

When Leslie was 17 weeks pregnant, she suffered from a premature ruptured membrane. In other words, her water broke at 17 weeks, and she lost most of the fluid surrounding her baby. Unfortunately, despite the doctors' best efforts, Leslie went into labour a few weeks later and watched her baby boy live for less than 30 minutes.

Losing her son was a wake-up call for Leslie. She was devastated and couldn't imagine going back to a role that didn't light her up. It was time for her to chase her dreams of becoming a vet. But going back to vet school was a huge commitment of both years and thousands of dollars and so Leslie looked into a job as a receptionist at a vet clinic right around the corner from her house. It was a great way to test what working at a vet clinic would be like—even if it meant leaving a well-paying job to make $14 an hour, work part-time hours and do things like answer phones and deal with unhappy or stressed customers.

While working at the clinic, Leslie got pregnant again and delivered a healthy, happy baby girl. Upon returning from maternity leave, Leslie took over as office manager and really got to see the ins and outs of working in a vet clinic. After her second daughter was born, she decided that going back to school for seven years to become a vet was no longer what she wanted. She wanted to have a fulfilling career but also to spend time with her kids. Watching vets in action, she realized it wasn't for her. Still, she was glad she pursued it, otherwise it might have hung over her for years. Now she had no regrets, and it didn't cost her thousands of dollars and years of her life to come to that realization.

By taking a break from the corporate world, Leslie had gained a new perspective of what she valued in a role and in a company. When she returned to the corporate world, she went to a role and company where she felt truly valued and fulfilled, working in the legal department for a technology company. The loss of her child helped her muster the courage to test the vet path as well as to realize what her priorities, values and desires were so she could align her career with them. Now she has found a happy balance between her work and her home life. It took her some extra time and some winding turns to get here, but Leslie is finally living her dream life.

In case you're still telling yourself you're too old to chase your dreams, here are some other more well-known people who pursued their dreams later in life:

- Julia Child wrote her first cookbook at age 50, which turned her into a celebrity chef.

- Vera Wang didn't enter the fashion industry until she was 40, after being a figure skater and working in journalism.

- Joy Behar was a teacher but then almost died from an ectopic pregnancy in her late 30s, before becoming a comedian and talk show host.

- Donald Fisher opened the first Gap store at age 40 without any prior retail experience.

- Betty White joined The Mary Tyler Moore Show at age 51, which put her on a path to becoming one of the most award-winning comedic actresses in history.

So no it's never too late. Just remember to believe in that beautiful vision that lights you up, take on the obstacles that hold you back, and keep going. Because you, my dear, are ready.

It's time to soar.

Exercise: Create Your Legacy

To help ensure that you don't end up with any regrets, I invite you to **write your eulogy or revisit the one you already have if you chose that from the Daring List**. I get this can be an extremely uncomfortable exercise as we generally dread thinking about our death, however I invite you to look at it as celebrating all of the great things you did on this earth, big and small. Use it as a guide to remember what's important for you to accomplish in this lifetime. It will help you understand what legacy you want to leave behind. How you want to be remembered. What's important to you at the end of the day. And if it helps, get your new definition of success out to check against it.

Once you have your eulogy, I want you to **write down your commitment to your vision of what lights you up and 5** *small* **action steps you can take** to get you on your way. Then I want you to commit to when you'll complete each action step and who can hold you accountable. Lastly, I want you to celebrate each action step as you complete them. You deserve it!

ONE LAST THING

"A bird sitting on a tree is never afraid of the branch breaking, because its trust is not on the branch but on its own wings."

–Charlie Wardle,
author of How To Sleep Better

I have one last story to share with all of you and that is my example of how I knew I'd finally found what lit me up. Because, let's be honest, there were multiple times in my career where I thought I'd found my "dream job." A lot of the time we don't know what lights us up until we try it. And if isn't the right thing, then we have to keep going until we find what is.

My wish for you is to have a moment where it becomes crystal clear in your heart and mind that you have found that light and that it is shining bright down upon you.

Here's my journal entry of when that moment happened for me.

You know what I did last night? I celebrated myself and shrieked with joy driving home from the airport. I was celebrating that I was flown to Saskatoon to speak at the Saskatchewan Workers' Compensation Board annual conference to an audience of 500 in between two seasoned speakers who've both appeared on TV and travelled globally, and I nailed it. Was it scary as hell? Absolutely! I felt sick for hours leading up to the event, but was it a dream come true? You bet it was! Knowing that I can help people to live happier and healthier lives is huge and the audience was incredible. Driving home last night I felt immense pride in myself for having the guts to chase my secret silly dreams. On top of chasing my dreams, I had finally found a way to feel proud without seeking external approval or validation. I felt it in my heart.

Now, friend, our time together has sadly come to an end (for now). Whether you've done all of the exercises here or plan to go back to them or not, it's OK. You have started your journey to break free and create the career and life you want and all that matters is you keep that vision close to you and you continue to take steps towards it.

No matter where you are in your journey, I invite you to celebrate. Celebrate finishing this book. Celebrate that you are on your way to creating and living a more authentic and joyful life. Celebrate you and all your awesomeness. Celebrate the incredible strength and confidence you have inside.

As you go forward, be sure to believe in yourself and in your crazy-amazing potential and know that you can overcome any challenges that come your way! The world awaits your unique brilliance, and I know you will shine bright.

I believe in you and can't wait to see you soar!

With love and hope,

Shannon

Let's stay connected!

Thank you for joining me on this journey to *Breaking Free*. If you've enjoyed the stories, tools and exercises shared in this book, I invite you to subscribe to my newsletter. Through my weekly emails, you'll gain access to exclusive content and offers, practical tips and inspiring stories that will empower you to continue breaking free so you can live a more authentic, courageous, joyful and meaningful life and keep shining like the star that you are.

Go to shannontalbot.com to subscribe.

Can't wait to see you there!

PS: If you enjoyed this book, I'd love if you could leave a book review on Amazon. Thank you!

ACKNOWLEDGEMENTS

I want to thank my Mom and Dad for their love and support and for never telling me what to be when I grow up or how to live my life. And thanks to my brothers, Bryan and Colin, for letting me openly share our story of loss and helping me fill in the missing details. We've had some great adventures together and I look forward to many more, including that camping trip we'll take one day.

Chris, you are my rock. Thank you for always believing in me and being such a great dad and husband. I can't wait to spend many more fulfilled years together.

Jackson and Zachary—just writing your names brings a big smile to my face and a warmth to my heart. I am the luckiest mom in the world to have both of you as sons. Your curiosity, intelligence, sense of humour and empathy are incredible and watching you grow is the biggest honour I have in my life.

I also want to thank my other incredible family members: Marcella, Jack (may he rest in peace), Angela, Nick, Matthew, Sholeh, Zephyr, Hugo, Denver, Donna, Jonathan and Alex. Plus, my many aunts, uncles and cousins. I love you all.

Adrienne Bartl–I'll never forget you asking me if I had considered writing a book after you attended one of my workshops. You walking me through the process of writing and publishing a book inspired me to finally chase my dream.

To my editor, Catalina Margulis, thank you, thank you, thank you. You are not only an incredible editor and book coach but you had my back every step of this journey and had a magical way of bringing this book to life.

To the wonderful people who let me interview you for this book–some, without even knowing me: Julie Cole, Stacey Mowbray, Victoria Pelletier, Monique Reddington, Lia Grimberg, Michelle Robertson, and the real people behind Amanda, Rachel, Serena, Nora, Leslie–you know who you are :)

To Amy Ballantine–thanks for designing such a beautiful and kick-ass book cover for me. You're so talented.

To my beta readers–thanks for helping me make this book even better: Allison Ayre, Afshan Razvi, Jennily Viljoen, Malwina Chaudhry, Nadia Daniell, Marie-Claude Turgeon, Tonia Djogovic and one more who asked to remain anonymous.

To Shantelle Melanson–you are one of the strongest, most positive, fun people I know. Thank you for being an inspiration to me and my biggest cheerleader.

To Darren Melanson–I'll never completely understand how you can catch every single spelling mistake or grammatical error out there but thank you. Plus, you've been a great supporter of mine for years.

To Jody Hyne–thank you for being such a supportive and true friend. I'm so grateful our kids introduced us.

To my high school gals–Angela Cantelon, Nicole Jermyn, Kim McCallum, Kim Westbrook and Sara Budnark–becoming friends with you in Grade 11 was the absolute best. Thank you for the wild but super fun times. I love that you're all still in my life.

To my university crew–Mara Lowrey, Christy Daniels, Christine Kapaklis, Kellie Chapman, Bobbi-Jo Stuart, Maggie Hubble, Matt Price, Dani Warshager, Jennifer Welsh, Marcie Sharpe, Tara Rhodes, Adrienne Bartl and Christine Moosbrugger–thanks for the great memories at Carleton and beyond.

To all my newer and incredible friends–thanks for sharing in the good and tough times: Leisha Vaughan-Humphreys, Jacquie Rashad, Michelle Russill, Janet Reid, Ashley Barnes, Andrea Barnes, Candra Reynolds, Naela Jinha, Michele Levey, Lara Watson, Justine Berezowsky, Carolyn Delang, Shannon Weir, Lily McNeil, Mo Reddington, Holly Bondy, Amy Ballantine, Miranda McKenna and Sarah Griffiths.

To my Peruvian (and Canadian) family–Barb, Alex and Catherine Dmitrienko, thanks for opening your doors and arms to me during my two years in Peru. I can't wait until we can dance to some more Rod Stewart tunes.

To my incredible bosses, colleagues and mentors–Gala Chan, Ed Mathur, Luce Veilleux, Anatol von Hahn, Rob Macdonald, Maia Simpson, Mary Jane Caleca, Mona Dakgi, Andrea Holmes, Johanna Schueller, Scott Kelly, Elizabeth Rosenfeld, Fiona Read, Jessica Moffat, David Hersh, Daksa Mody, Jason Ilagan, Laura Cooney, Leah Fantin, Rhonda Wooddisse, Jeremy Pallant, Jorge Lemus, Danny Llaguno, Dan McKenzie, Sharon McKenzie, Andy Saveedra, Raha Afkari, Radha Soni, Miguel Rodriguez, David Tee, Jennifer Hawkins, Joanne Azevedo-Vaz, Adrian Lang, Jess Montes, Catherine Parsons, Brett McIntosh, Lindsey Ash, Ali Klerer, Lindsay Loft and Tara Fremes. Plus, many, many more.

Lastly, to those who believed in me, either as a teacher or coach: the receptionist at the foot doctor (I wish I knew your name), Mr.

Smallwood, Mr. Kelly, Mr. Sutton, Mr. Scratch, Mr. Currie, Madame Turcotte-Lapaine, Margaret James, Sam Campbell, Adrienne Enns, Robb Gilbear, Saleema Vellani, Trevor Cape, Michelle Denis, Mark Black and Sylvio Deluca.

REFERENCES

1   State of the Global Workplace: 2023 Report, Gallup, gallup.com.

2   Horne, Moses & Troy. "Mental Toughness for Young Athletes." Buggily Group Inc. May 2, 2020.

3   Sarah Blakely, Candace Nelson episode 9. Shine On with Reese. Hello Sunshine. July 31, 2018.

4   Heal the Bay. "Vending Machines More Hazardous Than Sharks." August 2, 2013. [https://healthebay.org/vending-machines-more-hazardous-than-sharks]

5   Poll of 2,000 American adults by OnePoll with CeraVe. Survey conducted between April 16, 2020 and April 21, 2020.

6   Microsoft. *2021 Work Trend Index: Annual Report*. March 22, 2021.

7   Tara Sophia Mohr. "Why Women Don't Apply for Jobs Unless They're 100% Qualified." *Harvard Business Review*. August 25, 2014.

8   Saujani, Reshma. "Teach girls bravery, not perfection." TED. Mar 7, 2016.

9   Ohio State University: Fisher College of Business. "Why Most New Year's Resolutions Fail." February 2, 2023. [https://fisher.osu.edu/blogs/leadreadtoday/why-most-new-years-resolutions-fail]

10 Choi, Catherine and Laycock, Richard. "Americans spend $397 million on unused gym memberships annually." Finder. May 24, 2021. [https://www.finder.com/unused-gym-memberships]

11   Hall, K. D., & Kahan, S. (2018). "Maintenance of lost weight and long-term management of obesity." *The Medical clinics of North America, 102*(1), 183. https://doi.org/10.1016/j.mcna.2017.08.012

12   Parr, Chris. "Not Staying the Course." Times Higher Education. May 9, 2013. [https://www.insidehighered.com/news/2013/05/10/new-study-low-mooc-completion-rates]

13   Rizzo, Nicholas. Over 50% haven't read a book in the past year: 2022 Study. WordsRated. July 13, 2022. [https://wordsrated.com/american-reading-habits-study/]

14   Harter, Jim and Adkins, Amy. Employees Want a Lot More From Their Managers. Gallup. April 8, 2015.

15   Healthy Brains: Cleveland Clinic. You are your brain. [https://healthybrains.org/brain-facts/]

16   Lambersky, Sarah. "How to manage your 40,000 negative thoughts a day and keep moving forward." *The Financial Post.* October 16, 2013.

17   Rubino, Dr. Joe "The Impact of Lacking Self-Esteem." https://www.centerforpersonalreinvention.com.

18   Relationship Advice and Tools from Brené Brown and Tim Ferriss. The Tim Ferriss Show. February 9, 2020.

19   Jay Shetty's Podcast "On Purpose." Interview with Gretchin Rubin. January 11, 2021.

20   Survival of private sector establishments by opening year. U.S. Bureau of Labor Statistics. March 2022.

21   Clear, James. *Atomic Habits* (Penguin Publishing Group, 2018).

22   2022 Reno Report. HomeStars. June 22, 2022.

EXERCISES

ABOUT THE AUTHOR

Shannon Talbot is a Certified Health, Life & Transformational Coach. A former corporate leader in the financial services and advertising industries, Shannon started her own company, Shannon Talbot Coaching & Consulting, to help working professionals maximize their well-being and success and have more energy and joy across every area of their life.

Shannon has an MBA from the Schulich School of Business and has been featured on CBC Radio and in Today's Parent, Chatelaine, LifeHack and Thrive Global. She has helped hundreds of working professionals and dozens of organizations through her coaching and speaking programs.

Shannon lives in Toronto with her husband, two sons and dog.

www.ingramcontent.com/pod-product-compliance
Lightning Source LLC
Chambersburg PA
CBHW030904060726
47591CB00005B/1406